THE OFFICIAL UNDERGROUND
2012 DOOMSDAY
SURVIVAL HANDBOOK

COMPILED BY W. H. MUI

HOW BOOKS

Cincinnati, Oh:
www.howdesign.c

D0710124

THE OFFICIAL UNDERGROUND 2012 DOOMSDAY SURVIVAL HANDBOOK. Copyright © 2011 by Grant Murray. Manufactured in the USA. All rights reserved. No other part of this book may be reproduced in any form or by any electronic or mechanical means including information storage and retrieval systems without permission in writing from the publisher, except by a reviewer, who may quote brief passages in a review. Published by HOW Books, an imprint of F+W Media, Inc., 4700 East Galbraith Road, Cincinnati, Ohio 45236. (800) 289-0963. First edition.

For more excellent books and resources for designers, visit www.howdesign.com.

15 14 13 12 11   5 4 3 2 1

Distributed in Canada by Fraser Direct, 100 Armstrong Avenue, Georgetown, Ontario, Canada L7G 5S4, Tel: (905) 877-4411. Distributed in the U.K and Europe by F+W Media International, Brunel House, Newton Abbot, Devon, TQ12 4PU, England, Tel: (+44) 1626-323200, Fax: (+44) 1626-323319, E-mail: postmaster@davidandcharles. co.uk. Distributed in Australia by Capricorn Link, P.O. Box 704, Windsor, NSW 2756 Australia, Tel: (02) 4577-3555.

Library of Congress Cataloging-in-Publication Data

Mumfrey, W. H.
 The official underground 2012 doomsday survival handbook / W.H. Mumfrey. -- 1st ed.
    p. cm.
 Includes index.
 ISBN 978-1-4403-0817-8 (pbk. : alk. paper)
 1. Survival skills--Humor. I. Title.
 PN6231.S886M86 2010
 741.5'941--dc22

                                                        2010022823

Edited by AMY OWEN
Designed by GRACE RING
Illustrated by GREG NOCK

Dedication

For Rebecca. You can never be too careful.

Acknowledgments

Thanks to cinephile extraordinaire Adam Lampe for filling in a few blanks in apocalyptic movies of the 1950s and 60s. Thanks also to my editor Amy Owen, who never fails to make the editing process enjoyable.

ABOUT THE AUTHOR

W.H. Mumfrey lives on an island off the south coast of Australia and is ready to seal the bunker door at a moment's notice.

TABLE OF CONTENTS

INTRODUCTION

All good things come to an end: the summer holidays, your favorite TV show, the tub of ice cream you'd carefully hidden at the back of the freezer. Why should humanity be any different? Since the very dawn of time, species have risen and fallen with grim regularity. Organisms emerge from the primeval sludge, have their brief time in the sun, then perish along with the countless other creatures that preceded them. It has been estimated that 99.9 percent of all the species that have ever lived are now extinct. One day humans will be counted among that number. It's only a matter of time. Many now believe that day may very well be at hand. It is not the menace of global warming or other acts of environmental barbarism that we need fear in the short term, but a disaster of positively biblical proportions—a cataclysmic event that will have humanity clinging by its collective fingertips to the cliff of existence.

According to Mayan legend, our end could be as soon as December 21, 2012. Now, predictions of this kind are nothing new. Ever since our species swung down from the trees, there have always been party-poopers in the tribe that have warned that the good times are about to end. Yet, what if they are correct, and we are at this very moment hurtling toward a date with oblivion?

It is true that we live in perilous times. While our own personal extinction is only as far away as a momentary lapse of concentration on the motorway or fifty years of a hamburger-chomping, artery-clogging diet, riding the freight train to Armageddon with the rest of humanity is quite another story.

Forewarned is forearmed. There would be nothing worse than awaking on December 21, 2012, to meet your doom wearing nothing more than flannel pajamas and an embarrassed expression on your face. Let nobody tell you that they told you so.

This book is for those who do not want to perish with the masses on that or any other day. This book is for survivors.

SECTION 1

THE END IS NIGH... AGAIN

"All we see and admire today will burn in the universal fire that ushers in a new, just, happy world."

—Seneca, 65 A.D.

One day Chicken Little was walking in the woods when an acorn landed on top of her head.

"Oh my!" cried Chicken Little. "The sky is falling! The sky is falling! I must go and tell the king."

On the way to the palace, she told everybody she met that they were in great peril and that they should take immediate action.

We all remember this story from our childhoods. It is derived from the fable of Daddabha, from the fourth century B.C. Buddhist book known as the Jataka, and is a timely warning of the perils of hysteria in the face of perceived catastrophe. Doomsayers have been heralding coming destruction since our simian forebears first started bashing rocks together. To date, all prophecies of doom have failed. If we can learn to discriminate between truth and error, we will not only save ourselves from all the embarrassment of preparing for apocalypses that aren't going to happen, but we just might be able to get ready for the ones that are.

While many have dreamed of superpowers such as flight, invisibility, telekinesis or even immortality, most realize that these will forever remain mere flights of fancy. Yet there are those who walk among us and believe, to the very core of their beings, that they possess powers to see the future, or at very least, they know someone who does.

Imbued with such powers, most would seek next week's lottery results or delve into the tangled web of future personal relationships. But there are some who would use their precognition for more altruistic purposes. Like Bill Murray's character in *Groundhog Day*, who eventually used his foreknowledge for good instead of evil, they would use their gift to avert tragedies or warn others of coming calamity.

Prophets and their prophecies of doom are what concern us here.

Although a complete history of doomsday predictions is beyond the scope of this book, it is important that we gain an insight into the wonderful world of prophecy by an examination of some of the more notable predictions since the dawn of human records. For it is by learning from the mistakes of others that we will not be doomed to repeat them.

Like Noah before the flood, you will encounter many who doubt the soon-coming apocalypse. They will mock and deride your preparations. They will laugh as you warn those around you of their impending doom.

But remember, when December 21, 2012, dawns to whatever cataclysmic fate awaits humanity, who will be the one laughing as the perishing hordes beat on your reinforced bunker door?

2800 B.C., ASSYRIA

According to Isaac Asimov's *Book of Facts* (1979), one of the oldest surviving doomsday predictions comes from a clay tablet unearthed in Assyria. It reads: "Our earth is degenerate in these latter days. There are signs that the world is speedily coming to an end. Bribery and corruption are common. Children no longer obey their parents. Every man wants to write a book, and the end of the world is evidently approaching...." It would seem that nothing has changed.

CIRCA 1000 B.C., PERSIA

Zarathustra (also known as Zoroaster), the ancient Iranian poet and mystic, had his first vision at the age of thirty. This led to his development of a philosophy that ran contrary to the popular polytheistic religions of the day. Although at first he found it difficult to win any converts (except his cousin, Maidhyoimanha), his teachings eventually went on to form the foundation of a religion that is today known as Zoroastrianism.

The core of his beliefs revolved around a moral philosophy of choice. Those who pursue a good life through thought, word and deed will be happier than those who don't. Zoroaster also taught that at the end of the age of man, there would be a great battle between the forces of good and the forces of evil. The mountains of the earth would melt away and rivers of molten metal would flow across the earth, consuming the unrighteous. Only the just would survive. Zoroaster was a very wise prophet indeed; he did not give many specifics.

Zoroaster taught that at the end of the age of man, the mountains of the earth would melt away and rivers of molten metal would flow across the earth consuming the unrighteous. Only the just would survive.

634 B.C., ROME

The recent popularity of games like Sudoku demonstrates our strange fascination with finding number patterns in the world around us. From the very earliest of times, doomsayers have tried to join the dots in any way they could to help support their claims. More often than not, this would involve convoluted juggling tricks with mathematics and calendar dates. Often, with a little imagination and a huge suspension of disbelief, these calculations would be enough to fool not only themselves, but also anyone else lacking the skeptic's eye. Sometimes, if you look at something hard enough, you start seeing what you want to see, like animal shapes in the clouds.

The early Romans were not immune to these apocalyptic numbers games. According to one legend, Rome was founded by twin brothers, Romulus and Remus. After surviving an attempted murder and being raised by first wolves and subsequently shepherds, they petitioned the gods to advise them on their town planning decisions. After taking the sighting of twelve vultures as a good omen, they found the perfect site to found the city of Rome.

In later years, citizens of Rome hypothesized that the vultures clearly indicated the number of years that Rome would last—each bird representing a decade. Placing their collective heads together, they surmised that as the city was founded in 753 B.C., you simply need to add 120 years to determine when Rome would fall.

It didn't happen.

A quick recalculation ensued. The mistake was now obvious. One vulture did not represent ten years, as previously thought, but rather one month of a year. Each year has 365 days, so each day was

In later years, citizens of Rome hypothesized that the vultures clearly indicated the number of years that Rome would last—each bird representing a decade.

obviously meant to represent one year, bringing the new estimated doomsday to 389 B.C. QED.

Once again, it didn't happen. The avian apocalypse calculation method was promptly abandoned, and the Romans returned to more productive pursuits like territorial expansion. However, a precedent was now set and the way was paved for future doomsayers to test their mettle against the dull edge of the popular mind. This was not the first and would certainly not be the last apocalyptic prediction to fall short of hitting the mark.

167 B.C., BABYLON

The Book of Daniel recounts the story of the Jewish captivity in Babylon after the Siege of Jerusalem in 597 B.C. The hero of the story, Daniel, is forced to serve in the courts of a foreign king after being deported from his native land. After rising through the ranks as a part-time lion tamer and interpreter of dreams, he naturally becomes political advisor to the king. With more free time on his hands than he knows what to do with, he dedicates himself to recording a series of personal visions, which set the benchmark for all subsequent number-play shenanigans in apocalyptic literature. Biblical prophecies, being what they are, can often be somewhat difficult to interpret, as Daniel discovered when the Lord God gave him a vision of four mutant beasts, three aging tyrants, two haughty livestock and a partridge in a pear tree. According to the Archangel Gabriel, the meaning of these prophecies was so scary that they would remain a mystery until the very End of Days.

CIRCA 60 A.D., JERUSALEM

In the Gospel of Matthew, written towards the end of the first century A.D., Jesus of Nazareth fills us in on a few of the details surrounding the End of Days. "Countries will fight each other, kingdoms will attack one another. There will be famines and earthquakes everywhere. All these things are but the first pains of childbirth." "…The sun will grow dark, the moon will no longer shine, the stars will fall from heaven, and the powers in space will be driven from their courses. Then… they will see the Son of Man coming on the clouds of heaven with power and great glory." Although Jesus did not fall into the trap of giving an actual date for these events, going so far as to say that "no one knows when that day or hour will come," he did say that "all these things will happen before the people now living have all died." (Mark 30:11)

Understandably, many of Jesus' followers took all this literally and were disappointed, to say the least, when he didn't return as promised. Not to be put off by these minor details, each subsequent generation of prophecy-interrupting-Christian has continued to calculate the date of his return, usually within their own lifetime, for maximum marketing effect.

It must be remembered that Jesus was rather fond of speaking in riddles, which only the most discerning could understand

"...The sun will grow dark, the moon will no longer shine, the stars will fall from heaven, and the powers in space will be driven from their courses. Then... they will see the Son of Man coming on the clouds of heaven with power and great glory."

(Matt. 13: 10–13). "They look, but do not see, and they listen, but do not hear or understand."

90 A.D., PATMOS

Being locked up in solitary confinement for years can do strange things to your mind. And there are few things stranger than the account of the apocalypse found in the Book of Revelation. Purportedly written by the apostle Paul while in exile on the Isle of Patmos, this book records a series of spectacular visions about the End of Days. Unlike other accounts of the apocalypse in the Bible, these prophecies have everything: fire and brimstone, weeping and gnashing of teeth, and more numerical symbology than you can poke a stick at. This is what apocalypse is all about. God hasn't been idle all these millennia. He's been busy planning the homecoming from hell.

"Locusts came down out of the smoke upon the earth, and they were given the same kind of power that scorpions have."

Each detail has been lovingly crafted for maximum torment. Take the unleashing of the mutant grasshopper horde upon the unjust as an example. "Locusts came down out of the smoke upon the earth, and they were given the same kind of power that scorpions have. They were told not to harm the grass or the trees or any other plant; they could harm only the people who did not have the mark of God's seal on their foreheads. The locusts were not allowed to kill these people, but only to torture them for five months. The pain caused by the torture is like the pain caused by a scorpion's sting. During those five months they will seek death, but will not find it." (Rev. 9: 3–6)

But wait, there's more. God is only just warming up. Like Santa opening the toy-bag from the underworld, he has something for everyone: the oceans awash with blood, celestial bodies dropping from the sky, mountains moving from their places, darkness, death, destruction, mayhem. In other words, an apocalypse of Biblical proportions.

950 A.D., FRANCE

The spread of Christianity through Europe saw the steady rise of apocalyptic ponderings among those with idle minds. At this time, Adso, Abbott of Montier-en-Der Abbey, was requested to write a treatise on the Antichrist by Queen Gerberga, wife of Louis IV of France. In it, he describes how the End of Days will coincide with the last and greatest of the Frankish kings abdicating his empire before God and how the Antichrist will arise thereafter and oppress the righteous for three and a half years. During this time, two Old Testament superheroes, Enoch and Elijah, would be reanimated

During this time, two Old Testament superheroes, Enoch and Elijah, would be reanimated to fight the demonic hordes, only to be slain by the forces of evil.

to fight the demonic hordes, only to be slain by the forces of evil. Immediately following their deaths, the Antichrist will be killed in his tent, pitched atop the Mount of Olives. God will then wait forty days before judging the people of the earth.

This treatise was widely spread in Europe and became the most influential eschatological work of its time.

1186 A.D., SPAIN

In 1179, the astrologer John of Toledo calculated that the world would come to an end at precisely 4:15 P.M. on September 23, 1186, when a planetary alignment occurred in the constellation of Libra.

A letter was sent to Pope Clement III and other luminaries of the time informing them of the impending doom. It recommended that people abandon their homes and seek shelter in the mountains from the famines, pestilence, earthquakes and wind storms that would sweep the planet. News of this prediction spread quickly, with the Archbishop of Canterbury calling for three days of prayer and fasting to prevent the calamity. Just to be on the safe side, the Emperor of Constantinople walled up the windows of his palace.

Doomsday passed without event.

John's letter, with the names and dates changed, went on to become one of the first chain letters in history, circulating throughout Europe for centuries.

PROPHECY FOR BEGINNERS

Always wanted to be a prophet? Here's how. Being a prophet is more about smoke and mirrors and showmanship than divine revelation. Going from a nobody to "prophet of doom" can be as simple as following these four steps.

Step 1: Select an Impressive Origin

Announce your prophecy has come to you by way of a dream or vision or was directly bestowed by some form of higher entity. When dealing with concocted ethereal beings, extraterrestrials or deities, verification is always impossible. Matters of faith are incontrovertible.

Step 2: Think Big When It Comes to Content

Bigger is best. Don't hold back; the greater the predicted cataclysm, the higher the public interest. People stop to look at traffic accidents for a reason. Why focus on minor mishaps when mass carnage always makes the front page?

Prophecies are best written after the event and presented in such a way that they give every appearance of being given before. This way, you can be a lot more specific and get some impressive fulfillments under your belt at the same time. When prophesying future events, generalities are better than specifics. Write your prophecies in such a way that they could have multiple interpretations and be applied to one of any number of possible events. The use of symbols helps to cover your meaning, allowing others to read into your prophecy what they will. The use of complex number sequences is another sleight-of-hand trick that will give your prophecy an air of authority and so many possible interpretations that you are almost guaranteed a hit sooner or later.

Step 3: Amass Some Followers

Wherever there is a prophecy, there is somebody willing to believe it. Apocalyptic prophecies consist of the intoxicating mix of precognition and calamity. You will attract followers like moths to a light bulb as long as you have a marketing campaign to suit your target audience.

Step 4: Guarantee Fulfillment

Making a prophecy is the easy part. Its perceived fulfillment is a little more challenging. Focus on creating prophecies that can easily be matched with real life events, such as natural disasters or civil unrest. These happen on a regular basis and a properly constructed prophesy can be twisted to accommodate these sort of events with a minimum of effort. Don't be too specific about location and never pinpoint a date. If one of your more specific prophecies fails to eventuate, say that it was misinterpreted. People will be more interested in the one prophecy you get right, rather than the ninety-nine you get wrong.

1524 A.D., LONDON

In 1499, the German astrologer Johannes Stoeffler predicted that the world would be destroyed on the February 20, 1524. He based his prediction on yet another planetary alignment, this time in the constellation of Pisces. As Pisces is the astrological sign of the fish and fish are associated with water, it was obvious to Stoeffler that the earth would be submerged in a second biblical flood on that date. This prophecy was taken very seriously throughout Europe, with more than one hundred pamphlets being produced in support of Stoeffler's claims. Other astrologers were quick to come onboard, including the illustrious Italian soothsayer Nicolaus Peranzonus de Monte Sancte Maria. Boat builders across Europe were soon overwhelmed with orders for new ships.

In June of 1523, English astrologers, not wanting to miss out on all the excitement of this apocalyptic extravaganza, confirmed the predictions of an imminent deluge, but not wanting to follow in the footsteps of their European colleagues, pronounced the rain would fall on February 1, 1524, starting in, of course, London. True believers at the Priory Church of St. Bartholomew the Great, in London, immediately began preparing for the deluge by building an elevated fortress and provisioning it with two month's supply of food and water.

As the fateful day dawned, all eyes were trained heavenward. More than twenty thousand Londoners abandoned their homes and lugged their meager possessions to surrounding hilltops. The murmur of prayers beseeching deliverance could be heard as people jostled for higher ground. And then… nothing. It didn't rain that day. Not so much as a drop. In fact, records reveal that 1524 was a drought year in Europe. English astrologers announce their calculations are out by one hundred years and circle February 1, 1624 on their calendars.

Meanwhile, back in Germany, plans for February 20 were well under way. River banks and ports bristled with an armada of new boats, and local merchants stocked their shelves in readiness for brisk last-minute trading.

At the crack of dawn, Count von Iggleheim boarded his recently completed, three-story luxury ark. The crowds gathered on the wharf to watch the spectacle and jeer as his attendants drag provisions up the gangplank. Then they waited. It is more like an excuse for merriment for the assembled throng than the end of the world—until it started to rain. The crowd, fearing for their lives, stampeded; hundreds were trampled to death. Some, in search of sanctuary, stormed the assembled flotilla, including the Count's sizable vessel. The Count protested and was dragged screaming onto the wharf, where he was unceremoniously stoned to death.

The rain stopped and everybody went home, except the corpses.

Johannes Stoeffler made a few hasty recalculations and announced that the Great Flood was still on its way, but in 1528.

1694 A.D., PENNSYLVANIA

Drawing from an elaborate textual and numerological interpretation of the Book of Revelation, German-born writer and teacher Johann Jacob Zimmerman predicted that the world would come to an end in the fall of 1694, and the best place to view it would be the wilds of Pennsylvania. He was soon joined by forty others who shared his enthusiasm and started negotiations with the governor of Pennsylvania to secure suitable land for a settlement near ground zero. He envisaged building a community called the "Society of the Women of the Wilderness" in which he and his devotees (mostly men for some strange reason) would practice their arcane arts, including astronomy, astrology, geomancy and other magical forms of divination, until the big day arrived.

Unfortunately for Zimmerman, his own personal End of Days occurred while waiting for the ship to dock in Rotterdam.

Unfazed by this setback, Zimmerman's second in charge, Johannes Kelpius, took the reins and guided the Society to their new wilderness home at Wissahickon Creek. This mystic, musician and part-time troglodyte maintained Zimmerman's vision until the bitter end, which came with his death some fourteen years after the heavenly kingdom didn't descend out of the skies.

Mathematician Jacob Bernoulli predicted catastrophic results from the return of Kirch's Comet.

1719 A.D., SWITZERLAND

Learned mathematician Jacob Bernoulli (of Bernoulli numbers fame) predicted catastrophic results from the return of Kirch's Comet, the first comet ever discovered by telescope in 1680. Reputedly visible in daylight and sporting a spectacular tail on its first sighting, Bernoulli calculated the comet would hit Earth on May 19, 1719. Not only did this not happen, but the comet has yet to be sighted a second time.

1809 A.D., ENGLAND

While there are those who may question the use of astrology, sacred texts or visions to foretell Earth's future, who could possibly doubt a message of imminent catastrophe from a chicken? So found Mary Bateman (a.k.a. the Yorkshire Witch) who discovered, to her fortune, that there are few things that people won't believe.

At first, people were aghast; a chicken laying an egg on which was clearly written a warning of impending destruction? Surely it had to be some sort of trick or work of the devil?

But the Bible did have a talking donkey, and a divinely inspired goose once led thousands of peasants on a holy crusade to Jerusalem, so why not apocalyptic poultry?

The Chicken of Doom became an overnight success, attracting huge crowds, until one skeptic snuck in before the scheduled performance and witnessed Mary attempting to reinsert a freshly inscribed egg into a rather surprised looking hen.

The Chicken of Doom became an overnight success, attracting huge crowds.

The scam exposed, Mary moved onto other frauds, one resulting in a murder that led her to the gallows. Thousands paid to see her corpse, and the skin was flayed from her body, cut into pieces and sold as good luck charms.

There are some who say her talents as a thief, confidence trickster and compulsive liar were wasted on small-time fraud and would have served her much better in a political career, had that option been open to her at the time.

1844 A.D., UPSTATE NEW YORK

After experiencing the horrors of war as a captain during the Battle of Plattsburgh in 1814, farmer and self-proclaimed Baptist preacher William Miller announced that he had worked out when the world was going to come to an end. Using a complex and convoluted interpretation of cryptic Biblical passages, Miller calculated the long-delayed return of Christ would occur sometime between March 2, 1843, and March 21, 1844. After publishing his findings in a series of local newspaper articles, he soon had a devout following of believers, which were to become known as the Millerites.

When the heralded year passed without incident, a few in-flight corrections were made to their eschatological timetable and a new date of April 18, 1844 was set. Once again, the Savior didn't show.

Undeterred by these minor setbacks, skeptic turned Millerite preacher Samuel S. Snow had one last stab at it, proposing October 22, 1844. This date was endorsed by Miller, and soon the Millerites were once again whipped into an apocalyptic frenzy.

When the long-awaited day arrived, the Millerites, now numbering in excess of 100,000 people, trudged up surrounding hillsides and climbed onto rooftops to secure ringside seats from which to view the approach of Armageddon. Many, having given away their homes and possessions, had nothing left but the clothes they were standing in.

And there they stood, hour after hour, with arms raised and eyes heavenward, awaiting clearance for takeoff, until the clock struck midnight. Then… nothing happened.

The day became known as the Great Disappointment.

To add insult to injury, over the following weeks, the Millerites were subjected to public ridicule and, in some instances, violence. Churches were vandalized or burnt to the ground, congregations were shot at or attacked by angry mobs wielding knives and clubs, and one group was even tarred and feathered.

Five years later, Miller went to the grave convinced the Second Coming was still imminent. The Millerite movement spawned the Seventh-day Adventists, who are still waiting.

1874 A.D., NEW YORK CITY

Nelson H. Barbour, onetime Millerite, inventor and gold prospector, predicted Jesus' dramatic return in 1873. When this didn't happen, he fine-tuned the date to October 1874. Again, nothing. Not to be beaten by mere details, he decided that Jesus had in fact returned on that date, but the reason that no one had seen him was that he was invisible.

The following year, Barbour contacted Charles Taze Russell, one of the founding fathers of the Jehovah's Witnesses organization, convincing him that Jesus had returned the previous year, unseen by all. Russell, now carrying the apocalyptic torch, announced that

1881 was the new date. After another no-show, 1914 was announced, based on his calculations using Biblical sleight-of-hand and measurements from the Great Pyramid of Giza. Another correction soon followed—1918.

After Russell's demise, Joseph Franklin Rutherford laid the 1925 card on the table, stating that Abraham, Isaac, Moses and other Old Testament superheroes would return ushering in a new world, where millions would live forever.

Rutherford took up residence in a Spanish mansion in California, specifically built for the arrival of the Old Testament patriarchs. He remained in the mansion, holding it "in trust," until his dying day.

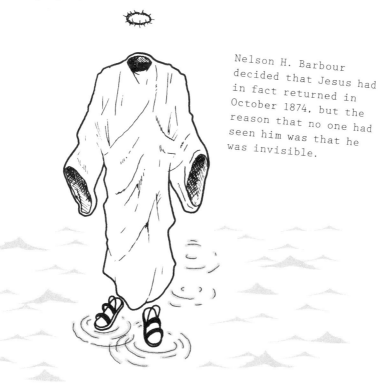

Nelson H. Barbour decided that Jesus had in fact returned in October 1874, but the reason that no one had seen him was that he was invisible.

1900 A.D., BRAZIL

Described by some as the quintessential doomsday prophet, Antônio Vicente Mendes Maciel, also known as Antônio
Conselheiro (Anthony the Counselor), was tall and thin, with "hair
down to his shoulders, a long tangled beard, an emaciated face
and a piercing eye"; he wore a rough canvas tunic and carried a
wooden staff, reminiscent of Gandalf from J.R.R. Tolkien's Lord
of the Rings trilogy.

After a failed marriage and short careers as a salesman and a
teacher, he roamed the Brazilian countryside preaching a message
of social reform to the rural poor and heralding the end of the
world in 1900.

Invoking the ire of both the Catholic Church and the newly
formed Republican Government of Brazil, the Counselor led his
followers to a remote rural location to establish a utopian community free from the tyranny of government oppression.

The town, called Canudos, soon reached a population of thirty
thousand, attracting landless farmers, former slaves and indigenous people from all over Brazil.

The government, feeling affronted by the settlement's newfound independence, sent in the military to teach them a lesson.

The Counselor's followers fought off three attacks before
being overwhelmed. Only one hundred and fifty people survived.
Canudos was burnt to the ground.

The Counselor died of dysentery three years before his predicted end of the world.

1900 A.D., RUSSIA

A cult from Kargopol, near St. Petersburg, by the name of the Brothers and Sisters of Red Death, believed the end of the world was coming on November 13, 1900. To celebrate the event, over eight hundred people decided to set themselves on fire. When authorities heard of the intended mass suicide, troops were rushed to the region, only to find that they had arrived too late to save a hundred people who had already self-immolated. When doomsday passed without incident, the rest of the sect dissolved.

1938 A.D., NEW JERSEY

On the evening of October 30, The Mercury Theatre on the Air broadcast Orson Welles's radio adaptation of H.G. Wells's *War of the Worlds*. An estimated audience of five million tuned into what initially sounded like a regular dance music program. As Ramon Raquello and his Orchestra played "live from New York Hotel Park Plaza," the program was interrupted by a series of increasingly urgent news reports of an alien spacecraft crash-landing near West Windsor Township, New Jersey. A field reporter described an alien emerging from the spaceship and opening fire with a heat ray, incinerating the surrounding people. This was followed by reports of the armed forces across the nation being wiped out during fierce combat with the alien invaders. Reporters advised people to evacuate the cities.

Many, tuning in after the show's introduction, believed they were hearing actual news broadcasts of a Martian invasion. Mimicking the style and feeling of early news bulletins, Welles successfully convinced as many as a million people that the end of the world had actually come.

A front-page article in *The New York Times* the following day describes how many listeners attempted to flee the city or hide in their cellars. A group of more than twenty families rushed from their apartment block with wet handkerchiefs and towels over their faces to protect themselves from the Martian poison gas. Newspaper offices and radio and police stations were flooded with thousands of calls from people across the nation wanting verification of the attacks or advice on how best to safeguard their

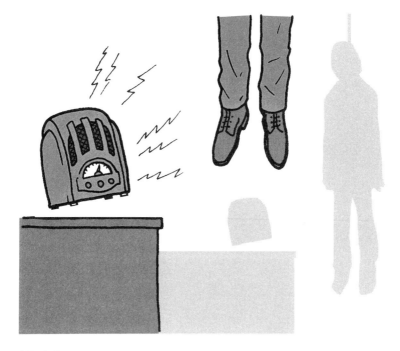

Mimicking the style and feeling of early news bulletins, Welles successfully convinced as many as a million people that the end of the world had actually come.

families. More than a dozen men and women were treated for shock and hysteria at St. Michael's Hospital in Newark.

When those fooled by the broadcast realized their mistake, they publicly derided Welles, who expressed regret that the program had caused so much upset.

1954 A.D., CHICAGO

Early in the 1950s, Chicago housewife Dorothy Martin discovered that she was receiving telepathic messages, in the form of "automatic writing'" from extraterrestrial beings from the planet Clarion. They told her that the earth was to be destroyed by a great flood on December 21, 1954, and that only those gathered in her living room on that night would be rescued by a spaceship and taken to another planet.

Martin soon had people knocking on her door wanting to reserve their seats on the alien craft. Many of her followers sold their homes, quit their jobs and left their families to demonstrate their commitment to their newfound beliefs.

The group assembled on the big night, awaiting the stroke of midnight. When the hum of landing engines did not sound out, they asked themselves what they had done wrong. Some reasoned that it was because they had not precisely followed the alien's instructions to remove all metal from their bodies prior to the spaceship's arrival: belt buckles, zippers, rings and bra straps had been jettisoned, but not tooth fillings.

Hours of weeping and soul searching followed until Martin received another update from Clarion telling her that their piety and faith had averted the deluge and they were all, in fact, heroes.

Extraterrestrial beings told Dorothy Martin that the Earth was to be destroyed by a great flood on December 21, 1954, and that only those gathered in her living room on that night would be rescued by a spaceship and taken to another planet.

The aborted space trip did not dampen the cult's spirits. Only two members left to try and rebuild their lives. The rest went on to either join or found other UFO cults.

The aliens told Martin to move to South America.

Leon Festinger's 1956 book, *When Prophecy Fails*, records the story of this UFO cult and proposes the theory of "cognitive dissonance" to account for the angst experienced after unfulfilled predictions of this nature. The term cognitive dissonance is used to explain the uncomfortable feeling caused by holding two contradictory ideas at the same time, such as wanting to live a long, healthy life and smoking; or believing in animal rights, but eating meat. In this case, when the doomsday predictions failed, the movement did not disintegrate, but rather, grew, as members justified their beliefs and became even more vehement proselytizers for the cause. This, yet again, demonstrates that you can lead a person to the fount of common sense, but you can't make him drink.

1974 A.D., LONDON

In 1973, David Berg, founder of the Children of God cult, predicted that Comet Kohoutek (C/1973 E1) was a sign of coming destruction in the United States, sometime during January, 1974. He warned his followers to flee the country before the dreaded month and take haven in others countries, specifically recommending Canada, Mexico, Puerto Rico or beachside hideaways in Hawaii.

Although hailed by the media as the comet of the century prior to its arrival, Comet Kohoutek turned out to be a dud, not being nearly as spectacular as predicted. When the only disaster to befall the United States during that year was Watergate (and that was more of a disaster for Richard Nixon than the country), Berg went on to predict the second coming of Jesus would be in 1993. Although he maintained that he received revelations from God that he would play a pivotal role in the much-anticipated Second Coming, he went to the grave in 1994 remembered more for advocating that his female followers share sexual favors with the men they proselytized in bars as a way of winning souls.

1980 A.D., MONTANA

Leland Jensen, chiropractor and third generation member of the Bahá'í faith, was expelled by the mainstream Bahá'í community and established an offshoot sect called Bahá'ís Under the Provision of the Covenant. He predicted a nuclear holocaust on

April 26, 1980, hiding with his followers in underground bunkers on that day.

He later predicted that Halley's Comet would be captured by Earth's gravitational field on April 29, 1986, and collide with the earth one year later. Didn't happen.

Continuing Jensen's tradition, colleague Neal Chase made almost twenty doomsday predictions during the 1990s. Basing his predictions on a mind-spinning concoction of Biblical, Hopi and Nostradamus prophecies; numerology; planetary conjunctions and dreams, Chase predicted everything from 9/11 (in retrospect) to a nuclear apocalypse wiping out one third of humanity.

1989 A.D., ORLANDO

Benny Hinn, stage performer, faith healer and televangelist, predicted that an earthquake would destroy much of the East Coast of America during the 1990s and that not one person would be safe. We can only assume that he used his considerable influence with the Almighty or made an offering of a small portion of his ill-gotten wealth to avert the calamity.

1997 A.D., JAPAN

The Japanese doomsday cult, Aum Shinrikyo (now known as Aleph), was founded by Chizuo Matsumoto (a.k.a. Shoko Asahara) in 1984. Starting as a meditation club, things soon graduated—as they sometimes do—to assassinations, kidnappings and murder; extortion and playing around with explosives; biological weapons and military hardware.

Asahara first predicted Armageddon would be in 1999, and then rescheduled it for 1996. Unhappy with the wait, some of his followers attempted to create their own.

Both sarin and VX (nerve gasses) were tested on hapless sheep on a remote rural property in Western Australia before being used in a number of assassination attempts in Japan. On the night of the June 27, 1994, eight people were killed and two hundred injured in an attack on the central Japanese city of Matsumoto. This was the first use of chemical weapons in a terrorist attack against civilians in the world.

On the morning of March 20, 1995, sarin was again released in a coordinated attack on five trains in the Tokyo subway system, killing twelve and injuring over a thousand others. On May 5, 1995, a burning bag containing a hydrogen cyanide device was found in a toilet in Shinjuku Station in Tokyo, the busiest railway station in the world. If the device had not been discovered and extinguished, it could have released enough poisonous gas to kill an estimated twenty thousand evening commuters. Further undetonated devices were found scattered around other subway locations in Tokyo.

Numerous cult members were arrested and imprisoned. Eleven received death sentences, including Asahara, who has maintained a vow of silence since the attacks.

1997 A.D., SAN DIEGO

Marshall Herff Applewhite, Jr.—music teacher, choir director, castrato and UFO cult leader—believed the earth was about to be "recycled" and that the only way to survive was to catch a lift on a passing flying saucer, which happened to be trailing in the wake of Comet Hale-Bopp.

While preparing for departure, his followers, sometimes numbering as many as one hundred people, lived a medieval-style monastic life, devoid of many modern comforts but relying heavily on technology to monitor their every move and earn an income for the group from website development.

Applewhite convinced many of his followers that they needed to shed their human bodies, by way of suicide, in order to board the UFO, which would then take their souls to "another level of existence."

On March 26, 1997, Applewhite and thirty-eight of his followers were found poisoned, each lying neatly on their bunk beds,

On March 26, 1997, Applewhite and thirty-eight of his followers were found poisoned, each lying neatly on their bunk beds, covered by a purple cloth, wearing identical clothes and brand new Nike athletic shoes.

covered by a purple cloth, wearing identical clothes and brand new Nike athletic shoes. Each of the boarding party had five dollars and three quarters in their pockets—presumably the fare.

1999 A.D., FRANCE

1999 was, of course, a year positively bristling with apocalyptic potential. With the lead up to Y2K (a.k.a. The Year 2000 Problem or the millennium bug—an unrealized digital catastrophe in which it was believed that computers around the world would crash as their clocks rolled over from "99" to "00" on January 1, 2000), doomsday aficionados whipped themselves into a frenzy with predictions of the immanent rapture, Earth axis shifts, doomsday comets, the second coming of David Koresh... 1999 had it all.

The potential of this portentous number did not slip past some of the more notable soothsayers of old. Of the more than

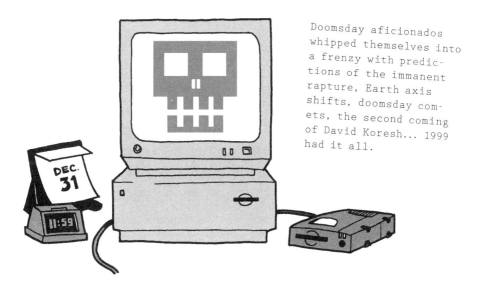

Doomsday aficionados whipped themselves into a frenzy with predictions of the immanent rapture, Earth axis shifts, doomsday comets, the second coming of David Koresh... 1999 had it all.

six thousand predictions he wrote in his lifetime, Nostradamus, prophet to the glitterati of sixteenth-century France, penned one that pertained directly to this year:

> The year 1999, seven months,
> From the sky will come a great King of Terror:
> To bring back to life the great King of the Mongols,
> Before and after Mars to reign by good luck.
> (quatrain X-72)

Despite the best efforts of Nostradamus' modern-day marketing department, the quatrain failed to successfully Velcro onto any significant world events during that year, leaving it forever cryptically camouflaged from those who would link the obscure to reality.

2000 A.D., EVERYWHERE

There's something about nice round numbers that stirs the heart of die-hard doomsayers. Needless to say, the year 2000 broke the record for the sheer number and mind-numbing variety of end-of-the-world prophecies. From the second coming of Jesus Christ and the war of Armageddon to the arrival of the Antichrist and the Rapture, all the way through to cosmic storms, solar flares, planetary alignments and the Y2K bug, the predictions for the year 2000 covered a lot of ground. Yet despite the complete failure of any of these predictions to eventuate during that year, the prophets of doom remained undeterred from their mission to warn the masses of forthcoming oblivion. Sights were set on greener pastures and the show went on; once again proving that the true caliber of a prophet is gauged not by the number of failed prophecies or the extent of their public humiliation, but by their ability to redraw their long bows and aim firmly at future events. After all, what are prophets without the future?

FINALLY

This catalog of doomsday prophecies is a testament to the tenacity and resilience of the human spirit in the face of constant failure. Time after time, predictions of destruction have been uttered from the mouths of the prophets, only to be recorded in the pages of history as being 100 percent *wrong*. But prophets are made of sterner stuff than that. While normal people would hang their heads in shame and sink back into the anonymity of the crowd, the true prophet rises to the occasion and uses these minor setbacks as object lessons for personal growth and future revelation. Despite the scorn and ridicule of intelligent society, they continue their work, undeterred, knowing that sooner or later, they will have to strike it lucky. If at first you don't succeed, try, try again. Without their tireless commitment to warning humanity of impending catastrophe, we would run the dire risk of being caught off guard when calamity does actually strike.

So it must be with infinite gratitude that we thank these purveyors of peril, for without their selfless dedication to humanity's future, we would remain ignorant of the Mayan prophecies of doom. Their persistence has, at last, paid off. This is the big one. Without a shadow of a doubt, December 21, 2012, marks The End of the World As We Know It.

A IS FOR APOCALYPSE

"No man has learned anything rightly until he knows that every day is doomsday."

—Ralph Waldo Emerson

I t is part of the human condition to wonder about the future. Each of us has one. Whether it be long or short, bright or gloomy, there is no escaping it. The best we can hope for is that we are prepared for our personal version of it.

The Maya were no exception to this innate desire to know what lay ahead of them. Using no more than the Stone Age technologies they had at their disposal, they constructed elaborate calendars and astonishingly accurate astronomical tables to predict far distant celestial and religious events of significance to their society.

Their obsession with these celestial matters permeated every aspect of their daily lives, being reflected in such things as their art, literature, religion and even their sport. From this fascination with the stars emerged a Mayan worldview dominated by the themes of ritual, death, the forces of nature and the cycles of time. It is the Mayan concept of time, or to be more precise, the end of time, that concerns us most. For if their interpretation of the universe is to be believed, then we have almost reached that point.

It is impossible to interpret the Mayan concept of the future without an understanding of the society in which it was conceived. For within each culture lies the key for unlocking its mysteries. And once unlocked, those mysteries may very well hold the key to understanding our own future.

ORIGINS

The Maya are probably the best known of the classical civilizations of Mesoamerica. Possessing the only known fully developed written language of the pre-Columbian Americas, their culture was as rich and diverse as any on the planet. Characterized by monumental construction and urbanization, the development of the arts, and the formulation of an erudite mathematics and astronomical understanding, the Maya were far more sophisticated than many cultures in Europe at that time. At its height, the Mayan civilization covered an area of some 150,000 square miles—from southern Mexico, Guatemala, El Salvador, Belize and Honduras.

According to American scientist Jared Diamond, the Yucatán peninsula of Mexico was first settled by the Maya around 1400 B.C., with the appearance of substantial stone structures around 500 B.C. and writing a hundred years after that. The so-called Classic Period of Mayan civilization began around 250 A.D., with an exponential growth in population, peaking toward the end of the seventh century. Then, within the space of only a few decades, cities were abandoned to the jungles and the breathtaking traditions and civilization of the Maya were destined to be no more than archaeological curiosities.

FARMERS AND KINGS

All civilizations ride on the backs of their farmers; the Maya were no exception. Art and science are not created on empty stomachs. An efficient agricultural system provides a society with an opportunity for some of its members to focus their attentions on things other than mere hand-to-mouth survival. With almost 80 percent of Mayan society consisting of farming peasants, it left time for the merchants, bureaucrats, soldiers, ruling class and all other sectors of the community to build the society that provided us with the key to unlocking our fast-approaching demise.

The Maya were no strangers to adversity. In many ways, the cards were stacked against them from the start. Corn, their staple crop, is relatively low in protein, and the hot, humid Mexican climate did not support its long-term storage. Unlike other developing Old World peoples, the Maya also lacked animal-powered transport (i.e. horses, donkeys, oxen, camels, llamas), which limited not only their ability to transport food and merchandise over extended distances but also their ability to reduce field labor with animal-drawn ploughs. Military campaigns were also limited to walking distance. This led the Maya to develop into small city-states headed by hereditary rulers, known as *ajaw*. Each of these city-states may have had a population of fifty or sixty thousand

Despite the Mayans' struggle against the odds, their civilization had drawn the short straw, and it was only a matter of time before they slid down the slippery slope to oblivion.

people and was no longer than two or three day's walk from the city center.

Add to this their lack of metal tools or the wheel, and it is astonishing how they created such extraordinary stone mega-structures, such as the stepped pyramid temples at Chichén Itzá, Uxmal, Palenque and Caracol.

Yet, despite their struggle against the odds, their civilization had drawn the short straw, and it was only a matter of time before they slid down the slippery slope to oblivion.

THE PARTY'S OVER

As is so often the case when you're having a good time, the party comes to an end way too soon. To their great surprise, the Mayan civilization discovered the same thing. As with the collapse of the Roman Empire, the disappearance of the indigenous population on Easter Island and the Anasazi of southwestern North America, one factor is never generally to blame for a civilization's failure.

One factor that has been identified as contributing to the Mayan collapse was population growth outstripping the available resources. Arable land around many of the Mayan urban centers was very limited. One Mayan city, Copán, located in western Honduras, had a population peaking around 27,000 people during its heyday and only 250 acres (one square kilometer) of fertile river soil to farm. The surrounding countryside was predominantly steep-sided hills with unproductive soil that was easily eroded.

The limitations of food supply and resource-transportation problems made it difficult for the Maya to develop into a united empire, as the Incas did. This resulted in chronic and debilitating warfare between independent city-states, which further taxed scarce resources.

This, together with a series of droughts, was the straw that broke the Mayan back. Water sources in many of the Mayan regions were unreliable at the best of times, but a severe drought turned the whole region into a dust bowl. The Mayan political leaders were about as unprepared for large-scale natural disaster as our own governments today. Between 90 and 99 percent of the Mayan population disappeared shortly after 800 A.D. The Maya's own apocalypse came a little sooner than expected.

Over six hundred years later, in 1525, the Spanish conquistador Hernán Cortés led an expedition through the former Mayan lowlands—the strongholds of Honduras—in search of the renegade adventurer Cristóbal de Olid. Although Cortés visited only one of the important Mayan centers, Tayasal, during his journey, he passed by numerous others, encountering only a handful of Maya, where once there had been millions.

GODS AND OTHER MONSTERS

The Maya, like some Europeans during the Dark Ages, believed the earth was flat and laid out in the shape of a square. Above the earth lay thirteen upper worlds, and below were the nine levels of the underworld, each with their corresponding gods. The gods themselves were as numerous and diverse as the various aspects of Mayan life they presided over. As with many mythologies, the Mayan gods lived complex lives, much like our own. They were born and died, became embroiled in conflict with their neighbors or fell in love. There was a deity for each aspect of life important to the Maya, including a god for death, thunder, rainbows, suicide, weaving and medicine.

Although there were more than one hundred gods in all, some, like Zeus, Shiva and Ra from ancient cultures elsewhere in the world, played a pivotal role among the deities. Itzamna ruled supreme as the creator god, who would manifest himself as Kinich Ahau, the sun god, during the day and a jaguar god as he traveled through the underworld at night.

Religious rituals and festivals were an intrinsic part of Mayan life. They were necessary to appease the gods and maintain order and balance in the world. During many rituals, Mayan nobility would wear costumes and masks to take on the appearance of the

According to some Mayan legends, it is a war god, Bolon Yookte K'uh, who will claim our world for his own.

relevant god. During such occasions, they were believed by the people to actually become gods. At other times, the gods were believed to manifest themselves through natural phenomena, such as thunder and lightning, rain, fire or even animals.

According to some Mayan legends, it is a war god, Bolon Yookte K'uh, who will claim our world for his own, unleashing the horrors of Xibalba, the underworld, upon us at the end of the 5,125-year-long cycle of the Mayan Long Count Calendar (explained in more detail later).

BE STILL MY BEATING HEART

Religion can bring out both the best and worst in human nature. When it is good, it is very, very good, but when it is bad, it is absolutely horrid. Just look at the Spanish inquisition or the Taliban in the medieval wastelands of Afghanistan. When power, intolerance and delusion entwine to form an unholy union, the bonds can strangle the life out of those in hapless servitude. When it comes to acts of barbarity, few can surpass those that profess sanctity.

Like many blood-drenched religions of the past, the Maya engaged in spectacular public displays of human sacrifice to appease the wrath of their vile gods.

Typically, a victim would be dragged screaming up the steps of the tiered temple pyramid and held down on a sacrificial stone slab by four burly priests. The high priest would then use a ceremonial knife, usually made from flint or

---

obsidian, to slice open the victim's abdomen before plunging his hand up into the chest cavity and ripping out the still-beating heart and holding it aloft before the delighted crowd. The defiled body would then be ignominiously hurled down the steps, bloody limbs flailing, to join the twisted mass of corpses piled waist-deep at the bottom.

This type of ritual sacrifice was common among the civilizations of Mesoamerica. According to some estimates, the Aztecs, considered by many to be the world champions at this form of execution, are reputed to have slaughtered upwards of eighty thousand prisoners over a four-day period during the re-consecration of the Great Pyramid of Tenochtitlan in 1487. That would average about fourteen murders a minute

Like many blood-drenched religions of the past, the Maya engaged in spectacular public displays of human sacrifice to appease the wrath of their vile gods.

during the four-day festival, giving both Auschwitz and the Colosseum, in its heyday, a run for their money.

Yet, even these gruesome public executions can become a little tedious after a while. To break the monotony, the Aztecs would vary the show from time to time. Decapitation and burning or flaying alive were popular party tricks, as well as pin-cushioning victims with arrows or hurling them into limestone sinkholes to drown.

Who better to comment on the end of all things than those whose expertise lay in bringing about the personal end of so many?

MATHEMATICS

It's all very well punching a few numbers into a calculator from time to time, but if all you had at your disposal was a paintbrush dipped in dye and a piece of parchment, many would find it a challenge to balance the domestic budget, let alone calculate lunar cycles over the next five hundred years. Yet the Maya did not only that but much more. Mayan mathematical ability was unsurpassed by any Stone Age culture. Using the symbol of a hollow seashell to represent emptiness, they independently developed the concept of "zero" nine hundred years before their European counterparts. While we use a decimal counting system based on the number ten, the Mayan system was based on the number twenty (the number of fingers and toes on the human body); this is known as a *vigesimal* system and was a key feature used in the development of their Long Count Calendar, which lies at the heart of the Mayan understanding of time.

Numbers were represented by a combination of dots, lines and a shell shape, as mentioned, to express the concept of zero. A single dot equalled one unit, and a line represented five. Unlike our own numbers, which run horizontally, the Mayan numbers ran vertically.

Petroglyphs depict Maya working on sums adding up to hundreds of millions and dates so large that it takes several lines of symbols just to represent them. This mathematical precision led to excellence in astronomy. They were able to predict solar, lunar and planetary movements and events with incredible accuracy solely from naked-eye observations.

PLAY BALL

With televised football still centuries away, the Maya dedicated themselves to a game called *pitz* with all the enthusiasm of Pittsburgh Steelers fans. This Mesoamerican ballgame is one of the oldest continuously played games in the world. Dating back to the second millennium B.C., it is also the oldest known game to use a rubber ball.

The ball was made from solid rubber, often weighing ten pounds or more, and ranging from a softball to a basketball in size. Diego Durán, the Dominican friar who observed games after the Spanish Conquest in the mid-sixth century, noted that players could be seriously injured when struck by the ball—often receiving severe bruising—and were sometimes even killed when hit in the head or stomach. At its most basic, players wore loincloths, but hip-guards and other protective gear were often worn to minimize injury.

The playing field consisted of a long, narrow alleyway between two sloping (or, more typically, vertical walls), enclosed on either end, to give it an *I*-shaped appearance when viewed from above. Court sizes varied significantly but averaged around 25 by 100 feet (8 by 30 meters). Games were usually played between two teams but could also be

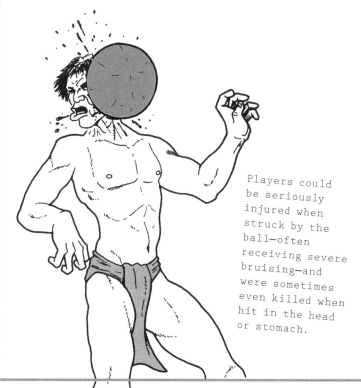

Players could be seriously injured when struck by the ball—often receiving severe bruising—and were sometimes even killed when hit in the head or stomach.

played by two individuals. Games were played on a social level by both women and children.

Although the rules of the game are not known, judging from its modern-day descendant, ulama, they were probably similar to volleyball, but without the net. Each team was restricted to one half of the court, and the object was to hit the ball back and forth until one team failed to return it. In the most widespread version of the game, the ball was struck with the hip, but many variations have existed, including the use of bats, rackets or other parts of the body. Points were scored for hitting the opposing team's end wall. Points were lost for allowing the ball to bounce more than twice; hitting the ball outside the court; and trying, but failing, to pass a ball through one of the two high, center-court, wall-mounted stone rings. A team won by successfully passing the ball through one of these rings.

Pitz was an intrinsic part of Mayan religious, political and social life, going far beyond being just a mere sporting event. In the late 1500s, the Franciscan Cardinal Juan de Torquemada noted that the game was used to settle local and inter-kingdom disputes; a game was often played instead of going to war. Mayan leaders would sometimes wage their fortunes or even their kingdoms on the outcome of games. Human sacrifices were commonplace at games, with losing team members often being decapitated before the crowd. Some have even suggested that human heads were sometimes used as balls.

WRITING

The earliest recorded Mayan inscriptions date back to around 300 B.C. Over the centuries, their writing developed into the most complex system found in the Americas and was in use for a hundred or so years after the Spanish gate crashed the party during the 1500s.

The Mayan writing system consists of a combination of hieroglyph-like symbols (known as logograms) which represent complete words, and a series of phonetic symbols. They were used together in much the same way modern Japanese uses Kanji (Chinese characters that represent whole words or phrases) and hiragana and katakana (syllabic scripts). The Mayan writing system is the only Pre-Columbian script known to completely represent the spoken language of the community from which it was derived. At any one time, up to five hundred glyphs were in common use.

Approximately ten thousand individual texts have so far been discovered, predominantly carved on monument walls

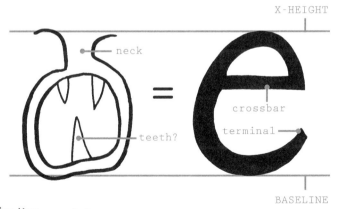

The Mayan writing system consists of a combination of hieroglyph-like symbols (known as logograms) which represent complete words, and a series of phonetic symbols.

or monoliths. Most of these are astrological records, calendars or information about the various ruling dynasties and religious rituals. Although the Maya also produced many written works on paper (called *amatl*), most were destroyed by the Spanish in a religious frenzy shortly after their invasion. Only three Mayan codices have survived to the present day. These represent only the tiniest fraction of Mayan records and leave us guessing as to the true complexity and richness of their culture. It could be compared to some future archaeologists basing their understanding of our once-glorious Western civilization on a couple of weathered *Sky and Telescope* and *Who* magazines.

Each of the surviving Mayan codices is named after the city in which it is now located.

Paris Codex

This codex was first acquired by France's Bibliothèque Nationale (National Library) in 1832. After disappearing for a number of years, it was "rediscovered" in 1859, by Léon de Rosny, in a pile of papers in the corner of a chimney at the library. Only a segment of the original document has survived—outlining Mayan ritual and ceremonies, with information on Mayan gods and history; astronomy, including the Mayan zodiac; meteorological and calendrical cycles.

Madrid Codex

Like the other two codices, the Madrid Codex is a concertinaed book painted on bark paper, coated in fine white lime. Once thought to be two separate works, this 112-page book was written around the time of the Spanish conquest and contains a description of the divinities and rituals associated with the 260-day Tzolk'in calendar.

Dresden Codex

Believed by many scholars to be the earliest surviving book written in the Americas, this 74-page, "screen-folded" codex was collected from a private owner in Vienna in 1739. Damaged during the firebombing of Dresden in World War II, what survives of the document has been meticulously restored and is now housed in the Sächsische Landesbibliothek (Royal Library) in Dresden, Germany.

This codex is the most important, strikingly beautiful and elaborate of all the Mayan codices. It contains incredibly accurate astronomical tables relating to solar and lunar cycles, as well

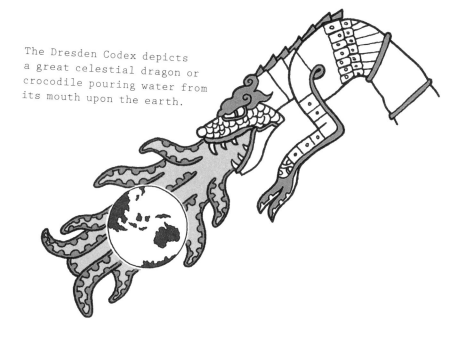

The Dresden Codex depicts a great celestial dragon or crocodile pouring water from its mouth upon the earth.

as planetary cycles, astrological information and religious tables. There is also information on medicine and meteorological cycles relating to agriculture.

These delicate pages also contain references to the end of the "fourth creation," the era in which the Maya believed man is now living. The codex depicts a great celestial dragon or crocodile pouring water from its mouth upon the earth. This, along with an image of the goddess Chac Chel pouring water from a jar, has led many to believe that if the world is not submerged in a global deluge in 2012, then at least we should expect some other global calamity. These predictions, along with a few monolithic petroglyphs depicting the descent of some transcendent entity to the earth, form the basis of the Mayan doomsday prophecies.

JUST A MATTER OF TIME

We've all done it: shown up to an appointment only to find that it was the day before. Now, just think how embarrassed you'd be showing up to the apocalypse on the wrong day. It is important that we get our dates correct, right from the start.

The calendar system with which we are most familiar is called the Gregorian calendar. Introduced by Pope Gregory XIII on February 24, 1582, it is one of the most widespread civil calendar systems used in the world today. Other currently used calendars include the Indian national calendar, Hebrew calendar, Iranian calendar, Islamic calendar and the Chinese calendar. Many countries use a number of calendars concurrently.

The ancient Maya also used a number of different calendars, each for a specific purpose. Two of the most commonly used were the 365-day solar calendar, known as the Haab', and the 260-day ceremonial calendar, known as the Tzolk'in.

Although neither the Haab' or Tzolk'in calendars recorded multiple years, if both calendars were used in unison they were sufficient to pinpoint specific dates over the period of a Mayan lifetime. As the two calendars were based on 365 days and 260 days, respectively, the whole cycle would repeat every fifty-two solar years. Together these two calendars were known as the Calendar Round, and it was sufficient for most Mayan's purposes, as life expectancy was generally less than fifty-two years.

The Long Count Calendar

For our purposes, it is important that we focus on the Mayan Long Count Calendar, for this is the one that tells us how many days there are before our apocalyptic Christmas. The Long Count Calendar was used by the Maya to measure time periods longer than fifty-two years. This calendar records the number of days from the date of creation, which according to the Mayan's calculations, occurred on August 11, 3114 B.C. (not October 23, 4004 B.C., as proposed by Archbishop James Ussher in 1658).

While our counting system is based on the number ten, the Mayan counting system was based on twenty. With a system similar to the numbers on a car's odometer (which runs from zero to nine), each period on the Mayan calendar runs from zero to nineteen before resetting to zero again.

The calendar itself is comprised of five sets of numbers. The position on the extreme right hand side of the calendar would count the days up to nineteen (0.0.0.0.19), then reset to zero. The place to the left of the first position would then increase by one (0.0.0.1.0), representing twenty.

This second position, however, is the only exception to the rule. Rather than counting to twenty before rolling back to zero, it only reaches eighteen. Thus, 0.0.1.0.0 doesn't represent four hundred days, but rather 360 days.

So 0.0.0.0.1 is one day, 0.0.0.1.0 was twenty days, 0.0.1.0.0 was around a year, 0.1.0.0.0 was about twenty years, and 1.0.0.0.0 was approximately four hundred years. This last unit was known as a *b'ak'tun*.

When the Long Count Calendar reaches 13.0.0.0.0, or the thirteenth b'ak'tun, on the December 21, 2012, it will represent about 5,126 years since the start of the calendar.

In the early 1700s, a Catholic priest by the name of Francisco Ximénez translated an ancient Guatemalan text known as the Popol Vuh or "Book of Community." It records the creation myths and legends of the Quiché people of the western Guatemalan highlands. It showed how the gods failed in their first three attempts at creation but succeeded at their fourth: the creation of man in what was known as the "fourth world." According to both the Popol Vuh and the Dresden Codex, the fourth world will come to an end on 12.19.19.17.19, or December 20, 2012.

The following day—winter solstice, December 21, 2012—the Mayan calendar will reset to 13.0.0.0.0. and mark the beginning of the fourteenth b'ak'tun (144,000-day period) of the human era. At this time, according to the glyphs on the final page of the Dresden Codex, destruction will literally be poured out upon humanity.

CASH IN YOUR CHIPS

Just as when our own calendar comes to the end of its yearly cycle on the December 31 every year and resets back to January 1, there are some who believe that this is all that will happen on December 21, 2012; the Mayan Long Count Calendar will simply reset and begin the fourteenth b'ak'tun, without any effect on our daily lives.

It is, however, the fool who says in his heart that there will be no apocalypse. If we believe that our modern society is here forever, then we may very well be in for a nasty shock. The collapse of past civilizations only emphasizes our own vulnerability to sudden cataclysmic events. Cell phones and fast food one day can very quickly give way to underground bunkers and spears the next. It's not really so much a matter of if, but when.

Cell phones and fast food one day can very quickly give way to underground bunkers and spears the next.

If we are to have any chance of surviving hell on Earth, then we must start taking action now to secure our future; for it is only by preparing for calamity that we have a chance of faring better than the Maya did when things went from bad to worse.

APOCALYPSE HOW?

"Now this is not the end.
It is not even the beginning
of the end. But it is, perhaps,
the end of the beginning."
—Sir Winston Churchill

We can't say that we haven't had a fair go. Humanity has been doing its thing here on Earth for the last few hundred thousand years. Species reach their "best by" date all the time. In fact, about one percent of species on the planet are becoming extinct every hundred years, so it's only a matter of time before our own number is up. It is then not so much a question of *if* humanity will one day disappear, but *when* the final curtain call will be. And as for how, the jury is still out on that one.

Although no one knows how the apocalyptic dice will fall until the dreaded day, it is possible to surmise how many sides the Dice of Doom may possess. There are only so many ways that civilization could come to an end, and most of these scenarios have already happened to varying degrees at some time during Earth's history. The chance of one of them happening again is really only a matter of time.

We must not, however, dismiss the possibility of an apocalyptic wildcard being thrown into the game—some cataclysmic event totally out of left field, which nobody expects. These are the scenarios that are not only most challenging to accept as being a genuine threat to humanity but also the most difficult to prepare for.

But if we can learn anything from human history, it is that we must expect the unexpected. Those who prepare for any contingency will be those who are most likely to survive.

SUPERVOLCANO

Planning to spend the 2012 Christmas holidays in the natural splendor of Yellowstone National Park? You may want to think again. Not far under the pine forests and hot springs of America's first and most famous national park lies a simmering mass of molten rock the size of Los Angeles that could very well mark ground zero for the coming apocalypse.

When most people think of volcanos, they think of ones like Mount St. Helens, which erupted in 1980 after being dormant for over 120 years. With the explosive power of one Hiroshima bomb every second, it created a barren moonscape that has still not recovered thirty years later.

Supervolcanos, however, are not conical shaped mountains but huge collapsed craters, called calderas, which are much more difficult to spot. They are formed when magma from deep under the earth rises towards the surface but is unable to break through

Not far under the pine forests and hot springs of America's first and most famous national park lies a simmering mass of molten rock the size of Los Angeles that could very well mark ground zero for the coming apocalypse.

the crust. A large magma pool develops just below the surface, slowly building in pressure until it erupts with a force equivalent to a small comet impact. Cubic miles of dust, ash and sulphur dioxide are ejected into the upper atmosphere, blotting out sunlight and causing temperatures to plummet, in much the same way as a nuclear winter. These volcanic winters could last as long as five or six years, disrupting ecosystems and causing crop failures that result in the deaths of billions of people around the globe, through starvation and war.

Yellowstone eruptions seem to occur on a 600,000- to 700,000-year cycle, with the current caldera being created by a devastating eruption some 640,000 years ago that blasted a 4-in. (10 cm) thick covering of ash over half of the United States. Early in 2007, scientists discovered that the floor of the caldera was rising at a rate of almost 3 in. (7 cm) per year. That's three times faster than has been observed since measurements first began in 1923. Although this crust movement, which increased earthquake activity and poisonous gas leaks in the area, may not necessarily indicate that Yellowstone is about to blow, there are dozens of sleeping super-volcanos around the globe that could.

When the Lake Toba supervolcano in Sumatra (Indonesia) erupted 75,000 years ago—with a force equal to one thousand Hiroshima atomic bombs every second—it blew more than 670 cubic miles (2,800 km^3) of rock and dust into the atmosphere, blanketing parts of central Asia with up to 20 ft. (6 m) of ash, and lowered global temperatures by about 40°F (5°C) for half a decade. Some scientists have credited the blast with the dramatic fall in global human populations at the time to less than twenty thousand people.

The Lake Toba volcano is just one of the more than forty doomsday volcanos around the world that have blown everything surrounding them to kingdom come in the past. While most are now extinct, Yellowstone is one of the exceptions.

Attracting more than three million visitors every year to admire the largest collection of geothermal features on the planet, few realize they are walking over the top of a volcano that is over three times the size of New York City. Technically, it only takes 240 cubic miles (1,000 km³) of magma to erupt to qualify as a supereruption. Yellowstone has more than five times that amount just below the surface. Whether it blows on December 21, 2012, or not, one thing is for certain: When it does, you don't want to be anywhere in the neighborhood.

ASTEROID

It is four days before Christmas, 2012. You have told the boss you are feeling sick and left work an hour early. On the way home, you decide to stop and do a little Christmas shopping. There's not much chance of being seen by anyone you know, and anyway, you could always tell them you had to pick something up from the pharmacist.

You pull a sweater on as you lock your car and dash into the shopping center. You don't really know what you want to get your younger brother for Christmas, but when you see the one last iPod, heavily discounted, on a display stand, you step ahead of another customer and grab it. Feeling rather pleased with yourself, you pay and then exit the store. You will return home victorious with the spoils of your expedition, secure in the knowledge that you are a shopping god, invincible.

With the gift-wrapped box in your hand, you wait at the pedestrian crossing for the lights to change. You start to think that you should get a burger before going back to the car, but when you see the green signal, you step off the curb. Before your foot touches the ground there is a flash in the sky, brighter than the sun. Then, in silence, you and everything around you burst into flames.

About thirty seconds after the flash, as you lie on the road, with the skin boiling off your body, you see a shimmering bubble of compressed air spreading towards you, in complete silence, out of the sky. As the shockwave hits, you hear a sonic boom and the buildings around you are blown to pieces, crashing into the street all around. An airplane falls out of the sky, slamming into the earth two blocks from where you lie, your skin oozing over the bubbling asphalt.

Any buildings still standing after the initial airburst are moments later pummelled by winds stronger than any hurricane that has ever existed on the planet, leaving a scene of utter devastation in its wake.

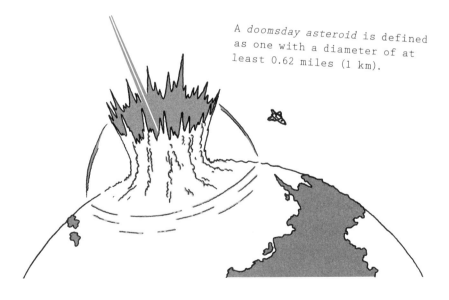

A *doomsday asteroid* is defined as one with a diameter of at least 0.62 miles (1 km).

You are at ground zero. An asteroid, 330 ft. (100 m) in diameter, has exploded in the atmosphere 15 miles (25 km) directly above your head. Although it's enough to ruin your day, this was not a doomsday event. Well, maybe for you and a few other million people who met their personal extinction but not for the planet as a whole. It will take a lump a little larger than that to bring on the apocalypse.

A *doomsday asteroid* is defined as one with a diameter of at least 0.62 miles (1 km). A really big asteroid, let's say 6 miles (10 km) in diameter, similar in size to the one that impacted the Yucatan peninsula, Mexico, 65,000,000 years ago, would unleash the power of a billion megatons of TNT, blasting enormous amounts of dust and sulphurous rock into the atmosphere, which would encircle the earth, igniting worldwide wildfires. Tectonic plates would be destabilized by the shockwave, creating unprecedented earthquakes and volcanic eruptions worldwide. The skies would be darkened for years; the environmental devastation would last for millennia.

But that's a worst-case scenario. The really big ones don't come our way too often. The smaller ones, however, are in plentiful supply. Again, it's really just a matter of time.

SPLASH

As 70 percent of our planet is covered by water, chances are an asteroid is more likely to strike an ocean somewhere than land. Recent studies have revealed that an asteroid measuring 660 ft. in diameter (200 m) striking an ocean 3

---

miles (5 km) deep would create waves over 1,000 ft. (several hundred meters) high, spreading out from the impact zone. Unlike tsunamis, which maintain their power under the surface of the ocean and then increase in height as they approach land, these waves would start breaking immediately, soon losing their initial height. By the time the waves have traveled about 20 miles (30 km) from the impact site, they will have shrunk to less than 200 ft. (60 m) in height. At the 600-mile (1000 km) mark, they would be less than 30 ft. (10 m) high.

Any impact near a major population center would, of course, be catastrophic, with ferocious winds and vast amounts of water falling directly from the sky. A 660-ft. (200 m) asteroid would splash billions of tons of water into the air, which would fall within seconds as an incredible deluge within 12 miles (20 km) of the impact site.

SOLAR SUPERSTORM

This apocalypse will be beautiful, at first.

It is midnight, December 21, 2012, and the skies above Manhattan are clear and filled with the flickering curtains of colored light. Uncommon at this latitude, the Aurora Borealis has set the heavens ablaze since sunset with a display that is simply breathtaking. Great swathes of light writhe from horizon to horizon, like a celestial pit full of giant incandescent serpents. Earlier in the evening, the news anchor had said that it was the best display of the Northern Lights since 1859. Parents bundled their children out onto balconies to see the silent phenomena, to a delighted chorus of "ooh" and "ahh." As the clock chimes midnight, New Yorkers coming home from late-night Christmas shopping or those still at their Mayan Apocalypse parties continue to gaze up at the night sky in awe.

Then, one minute later, the lights in the surrounding buildings flicker momentarily and go out. Everything is dark. Within another minute, large parts of the United States are without power. The grid is going down, enveloping the whole nation in darkness. There is no Internet or TV. Cell phones are reading "no service," and the only sound on your battery-powered radio is static.

Within a year, millions have died from starvation and civil unrest across North America alone, and the global economy is back to the Iron Age. Western civilization's heavy reliance on technology has led to its sudden demise. In one day, the sun has taken back what has taken mankind hundreds of years to achieve. Civilization, as we know it, has come to an end.

The sun is big—really big. At over 870,000 miles wide (1.4 million km), well over a million Earths could fit inside its bulk. The total energy radiating from the sun averages 383 billion trillion kilowatts, or the equivalent energy generated by 100 billion tons of TNT exploding every second.

Activity on the sun waxes and wanes during a twelve-year cycle, with the next active phase, known as a *solar maximum* (or solar max), occurring around 2012. The chaotic motion of charged particles on the surface of the sun creates magnetic fields that twist and turn around the sun, occasionally releasing vast waves of plasma, known as *coronal mass ejections* (CME). These CMEs can carry up

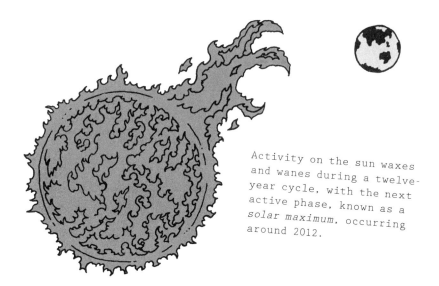

Activity on the sun waxes and wanes during a twelve-year cycle, with the next active phase, known as a *solar maximum*, occurring around 2012.

to 10 billion tons of electrified gas towards the earth at speeds as high as 1,200 miles per second (2,000 km/s).

Earth is largely protected from the usual stream of charge particles from the sun, called the solar wind, by the magnetosphere, a bubble of magnetism surrounding the planet. But sometimes this force field can be overwhelmed by the sheer volume of a CME, opening the magnetosphere like a can opener and allowing plasma to pour into the atmosphere. The ensuing geomagnetic storm could create power surges that knock out communications satellites and fry transformers, cutting power to whole continents at a time.

The impact of power outages would soon be felt on the nation's interdependent infrastructures—all of which rely on electricity—including water distribution, along with heating/air conditioning and sewage disposal; transportation and fuel supplies; financial markets, etc. Supermarket shelves would not be replenished and be bare within two days. The modern healthcare system would grind to a halt as hospital generators ran out of fuel and then pharmaceuticals within a week.

Replacing burnt out transformers would take months or even years, as few replacement parts are stockpiled and must be made to order by factories that also require electricity to make them. Even when new transformers are operational, they may not have the number of specialized crews required to fit them.

There would be no cavalry coming to save the day, as every country around the world would be in the same boat. It is estimated that a recovery time of 4–10 years could be expected, but even then there is no guarantee that the United States or any other advanced industrial nation would ever recover.

GAMMA-RAY BURST

Seventy-five billion years ago, when our earth and sun were yet unformed, a star died half way across the universe. This massive star, which now goes by the romantic name of GRB 080319B, ran out of fuel, its core collapsing to form an extremely dense object known as a black hole. This process released an enormous burst of high-energy gamma rays and particle jets that tore through space at nearly the speed of light. As these jets ploughed through surrounding interstellar clouds, they heated gas, creating a bright afterglow, which for a few seconds was a million times brighter than all the light in the entire galaxy. By sheer coincidence, the jet of material shot out from this dying supernova directly towards the earth and, having traveled 75 million light years to reach us, was the brightest object ever observed by humans in the universe. In fact, when seen by astronomers on March 19, 2008 (which by a strange coincidence was the same day that the acclaimed science-fiction author Arthur C. Clarke died), the flash was 2.5 million times more luminous than the brightest supernova ever recorded on Earth. Although, to the naked eye it would have appeared no larger than a small star that blinked on for 40 seconds then disappeared again.

Had that star been in our own neck of the galactic woods, we would have been in serious trouble indeed. Typically a gamma-ray burst will only last a few seconds. Most of these rays would be absorbed by our atmosphere. The small percentage of the rays that actually reach the ground would have an impact on living organisms, but only a small one.

A much more serious matter would be the effect of gamma rays on the gases that make up our atmosphere. Nitrogen and oxygen molecules would be ripped apart, forming a toxic brew of nitrogen oxides, including nitrogen dioxide, the fowl-smelling brown gas that forms smog. This would have the effect of blocking sunlight and cooling the earth in much the same way as a nuclear winter. This nitrogen dioxide would eventually fall from the skies as acid rain, with severe effects on ecosystems around the globe.

Nitrogen dioxide would also have the effect of destroying the ozone layer, in much the same was as chlorofluorocarbons (CFCs). The ozone layer is responsible for shielding life on Earth from the sun's dangerous ultraviolet light. With up to 50 percent of this protective shield destroyed by a GRB (the recent CFC-created holes resulted in only a 5 percent depletion), life on Earth would be exposed to massive doses of UV radiation from our own sun over the following decade. This ultraviolet influx would make plant growth almost impossible and increase the rate of cancer to animals exposed to direct sunlight. Whole ecosystems would collapse and food production would stop. Billions would die of starvation within six months.

Another immediate damaging effect would come from the UV flash that accompanies the GRB. Although this would again be limited to the side of the earth facing the blast, it would have a significant impact, damaging DNA and eventually killing a large number of living organisms exposed to the flash both on land and in shallow seas.

Gamma ray bursts can damage DNA, eventually killing a large number of living organisms exposed to the flash both on land and in shallow seas.

Although the gamma-ray burst may only last a fraction of a second, cosmic rays may shower the planet for centuries. Cosmic rays are high-energy particles, mostly protons, originating from supernova shockwaves. The earth is already constantly showered in cosmic rays, most of which are absorbed in the upper atmosphere. A number of secondary particles are produced as the result of their interaction with the chemicals of the upper atmosphere. Muons, for example, would not only irradiate the earth's surface, but also penetrate deep underground, effectively leaving nowhere to hide.

At sea level, we are exposed to the equivalent of about ten chest X-rays a year from these cosmic rays and their secondary particles, resulting in around one hundred people dying of cancer worldwide. This is all part of the natural background radiation to which we are all exposed and not something to be overly concerned about. A cosmic ray storm is, however, quite another story. Some scientists believe that the cosmic-ray-induced mutations from mega-GRBs may have been responsible, in part, for mass extinction in the past, where up to 70 percent of life on Earth perished.

Although stars capable of producing a GRB are rare in our immediate galactic neighborhood, they are not altogether nonexistent. One candidate is an enormous star, called WR104, 8,000 light-years away in the constellation of Sagittarius. Its rotational axis is aligned within 16° of Earth, which means that if it were to explode, it could jettison a GRB directly at us. Unfortunately there is no way of knowing if one is already on its way, and even if we knew, there would not be a lot we could do about it.

PARTICLE ACCELERATOR

Since man first wielded a sharpened stick against his tribal foe, he has been thinking of bigger and better ways to impose his will on those who don't share his opinions. Not only has mankind shown a particular gift for violence, but it has demonstrated that with ingenuity and perseverance, perfection of the art may be achieved. It is not unthinkable to imagine the clash of egos one day leading to nuclear exchange. Dogma and technology are always a toxic mix.

Yet, it may not be the religious and ideological zealots that we need to worry about. Science may inadvertently lead us to our doom with soothing reassurances and guarantees of a brighter future for humanity. It may be a case of "Whoops… apocalypse!" rather than some premeditated act of lunacy that destroys the planet. We have always known that men who wear suits are villains, but maybe it's the bespectacled guys in lab coats that we need to keep our eyes on.

There are those who believe that a doomsday device not only exists, but is being primed at this very moment to conduct "experiments" that will devour the earth in one of any number of bizarre ways.

The Large Hadron Collider (LHC) is the largest and most powerful particle accelerator in the world today. Buried deep under the Alps along the Swiss-French border, this "atom smasher," as they were called in the 1940s, may hold the key to understanding what the universe was like one billionth of a second after the big bang, 13.7 billion years ago.

Hailed as the most expensive machine ever built, the LHC is housed in a 17-mile (27 km) long circular tunnel, holding two pipes enclosed within a ring of liquid-helium-cooled superconducting magnets. These magnets are used to accelerate atomic particles to within a hairsbreadth of the speed of light (99.999999 percent of the speed of light, to be precise), before smashing them into one another to see what happens. The particles created by these impacts, many of which only exist for one thousandth of a billionth of a billionth of a second, are captured by an enormous (some as high as a seven-story building), complex series of detectors set in cathedral-sized caverns, located at strategic points around the tunnel.

The beauty of the experiments conducted on this extraordinary machine is that, unlike the Big Bang itself, they can be repeated over and over again, and examined in minute detail. Through these experiments, scientists hope to uncover the nature of the

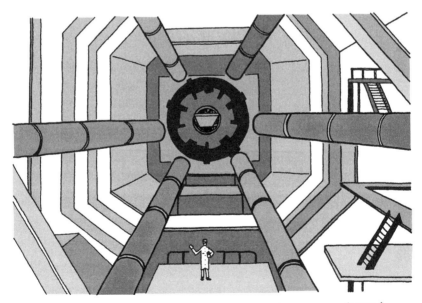

There are some who believe that the experiments conducted on the Large Hadron Collider may put the very existence of Earth in jeopardy.

fundamental particles that make up the very stuff of which the universe is made.

However, there are some who believe that these experiments may put the very existence of Earth in jeopardy. If things go wrong, then any number of very nasty things could happen.

Some have suggested that the LHC could create theoretical particles called *strangelets*. It is theorized that when a strangelet comes in contact with ordinary matter, from which Earth is made, it could convert the ordinary matter into strange matter. An uncontrollable chain-reaction would then be set in motion that would see the world we know consumed and reborn as "strange-planet."

Others believe that microscopic black holes could be created that will burrow down to the center of the earth and slowly eat our planet from the inside out.

The collapse of quantum vacuum is another contender for a particle-accelerator apocalypse. There has been some speculation amongst physicists that the universe may not be in its most stable configuration, and that the LHC may produce a "bubble" of a more stable, lower-energy state, which will expand to devour the earth and eventually the entire universe.

Still another concern is the creation of magnetic monopoles. These theoretical particles have only one magnetic charge, either a north pole or a south pole. It is thought that if created, they could become ravenous proton-eating monsters that would consume the earth one atom at a time.

Although scientists are quick to rule out the possibility of any of these things happening, one thing is for certain: When this smash lab fires up, it's going to be interesting whichever way the penny drops.

DAY OF JUDGEMENT

He's making a list and is checking it twice. Gonna find out who's naughty and nice. Jesus Christ is coming to town. It's been a long wait, but the carpenter's son has eventually come back to stake his claim. But this time, it's not gentle Jesus, meek and mild (where did that get him on his last visit?); this time he's coming to settle a few old scores, slip off the sandal and kick some ass. This time he's bringing some serious firepower with him: his Dad.

Now, God the Father is no stranger to violence. Although never averse to striking down the odd individual who irritates him, he really comes into his own when wielding death on a monumental scale. When it comes to laying waste the nations, no ancient deity even comes close. We need go further than the Old Testament body count to confirm his credentials. If the annihilation of humanity with fire and brimstone is what you want, then who ya gonna call? Jehovah!

The Lord's portfolio of carnage is as diverse as any third-world dictator's; from giant hail storms to the sword-wielding Angel of Death, he has all bases covered. We need only look at Noah's aquatic adventures to see what happens when God gets really annoyed. Yet, the Lord is not one for repeat performances. This time he's preparing a farewell barbeque; bring your own ribs and steak.

According to the Book of Revelation, the Lord has quite a few party tricks up his sleeve before the big sausage-sizzle begins. The prelude to Armageddon will include a veritable smorgasbord of environmental disasters, including toxic tides, solar discharges, famine, pestilence, mega-earthquakes, perennial darkness and meteor showers. No expense has been spared preparing the grand

If the annihilation of humanity with fire and brimstone is what you want, then who ya gonna call? Jehovah!

finale of arguably the most spectacular theatrical event ever staged. Each production detail has been lovingly handcrafted and guaranteed to create memories to last a lifetime—which may very well be only as far away as the weekend.

But hurry. Gallery seats are limited. This is definitely not something you'll want to view from ground level. The Lord expects prompt replies to his RSVPs and doesn't take snubbing his party invitations very lightly. The only question is: Do you really want to live next to Ned Flanders for eternity?

MAGNETIC POLE SHIFT

Although the magnetic north pole has long served as a reference point for intrepid explorers, the earth's magnetic field is anything but static. The magnetic pole had randomly drifted by as much as a few compass degrees over the last two hundred years, and if heralded changes are anything to go by, then Father Christmas may soon be relocating to the Antarctic.

There are many geophysicists who believe that we may soon be facing a polar reversal. Studies of magnetic-field records have revealed that there has been a steady decline in the strength of the earth's magnetic field since the 1840s. With the field declining at a rate of roughly 5 percent per hundred years, there is evidence to suggest that a pole reversal could be imminent.

The earth's magnetic field has flipped many times in the last billion years, according to the geological records. On average, the position of the magnetic poles completely reverses about once every 500,000 years or so. With the last pole shift happening 780,000 years ago, we are now well overdue for another one.

Although these pole-shift transitions generally take more than five thousand years to complete, scientists have recently discovered that magnetic flips can happen so suddenly that you could almost watch the needle of your compass move.

Analysis of magnetized rock samples from various sites around the globe has revealed that full magnetic-field reversals may take as little as two to three hundred years. One site, at Steens Mountain, Oregon, even revealed a 6° change occurring in just under two weeks.

Earth's magnetic field behaves in much the same way as a giant bar magnet aligned roughly along the axis of rotation. While the center of the earth is solid iron, the outer 1,500 miles (2,400 km) surrounding the core are made of molten iron. This outer core is constantly in motion, rising towards the mantle and then falling back towards the core again as it cools. These internal convection currents, along with the rotation of the earth, form a giant dynamo that generates a geomagnetic field.

Waves of magnetism swell out from the poles and loop around the planet like a giant bubble. This magnetic field extends beyond the bounds of our atmosphere into space, forming what is known as the magnetosphere. It is the magnetosphere that forms a protective shield against the waves of charged particles that are constantly bombarding the earth from the sun.

Apart from affecting compasses and upsetting the navigation systems of a few billion migratory birds and mammals around the planet, a pole shift has the potential to create far greater problems for humanity. As mentioned before, the earth's magnetic field acts as a protective buffer zone against the charged particles from the sun. The magnetosphere usually extends out about 60,000 km from Earth's surface. However, during a pole reversal, the

Apart from affecting compasses and upsetting the navigation systems of a few billion migratory birds and mammals around the planet, a pole shift has the potential to create far greater problems for humanity.

magnetosphere would dwindle to about 10 or 20 percent of its usual strength, allowing the solar winds to sweep over the surface of our planet. Even with our magnetosphere switched to "full protection mode," solar storms have the potential to wipe out global power supplies and communications. With our protective shields down, the results could be catastrophic to our technology-driven society.

SHIELDS DOWN, CAPTAIN

NASA recently discovered a hole in the magnetosphere ten times larger than anything previously seen. The breach was four times the size of Earth itself, opening up the entire dayside of the magnetosphere to assault from charge particles from the sun. Breaches of this nature set the stage for ferocious geomagnetic storms by loading the magnetosphere with twenty times the normal amount of charged plasma from the sun. Luckily for us, the breach occurred during a period of solar inactivity. If holes of this magnitude appear in our magnetic shield during the next solar max in 2012, then we could be in for one of the largest geomagnetic storms in human history.

PANDEMIC

Contrary to popular opinion, our planet is ruled by microbes. In fact, there are more microbes on Earth than there are stars in the universe (5 million-trillion-trillion microbes vs. 7 thousand-billion-billion stars). Since first appearing on Earth 3.5 billion years ago, they have permeated every possible environment on our globe. Together, they outweigh the collective weight of all other living things on the planet. There are ten times more microbes living inside the human body than there are human cells. The human digestive tract alone holds more than 3 lbs. of bacteria. Without them, we would not survive. With them, we may not survive either.

While supervolcanoes and asteroids would mark a spectacular end to civilization, these microbes pose a far more immediate threat to humanity. During the twentieth century, more than 100 million people died in three flu pandemics alone. That's around the same number of deaths that occurred in both World Wars combined. Yet that is only a drop in the bucket compared with the carnage these invisible beasties are capable of. While the Spanish flu virus

Today, with the fluid movement of people between countries, an infectious disease could spread worldwide within weeks, killing billions.

had almost a 3 percent mortality rate, Severe Acute Respiratory Syndrome (SARS) was close to 10 percent and H5N1 was around 50 percent, Ebola kills up to 90 percent of those who catch it. It is not hard to imagine how any one of these pathogens could mutate into an airborne contagion that could make the Black Death look like a runny nose. The Bubonic Plague was responsible for killing up to half the European populations it infected over a four-year period during the fourteenth century. Today, with the fluid movement of people between countries, an infectious disease of a similar magnitude could spread worldwide within weeks, killing billions.

ALIEN INVASION

General Douglas MacArthur knew only too well that one day we would face the "ultimate conflict between a united human race and the sinister forces of some other planetary galaxy" (October 8, 1955). If the UFO reports of the last seventy years are anything to go by, then they are already here, waiting for the opportune time to launch their attack.

Shining like a beacon in the cold wastelands of deep space, it comes as no surprise that our planet is a prime target for alien interest. With an enviable climate and an abundance of natural resources, Earth is a veritable treasure trove for the intergalactic traveler.

While the exact nature of an alien invasion will remain a mystery until the launch of hostilities, we can only assume that they will leave nothing to chance. Having monitored our defense systems and military tactics for decades, they will be aware of the considerable chinks in our armor and be both willing and able to exploit them mercilessly.

With an enviable climate and an abundance of natural resources, Earth is a veritable treasure trove for the intergalactic traveler.

Whether they come with all guns blazing or infiltrate our population, one identical replicant at a time, we can expect society to disintegrate swiftly before their technically superior war machine. It will be every man or woman for themselves when you find yourself in the sights of their laser blasters.

Although an alien invasion is far from the top of the potential threat lists of most doomsday aficionados, it must be remembered that it the horse with the longest odds that catches most people off guard when it gallops across the finish line. Fail to prepare at your own peril.

GLOBAL DELUGE

No preview of the upcoming apocalyptic would be complete without the aquatic doomsday foreshadowed in the Mayan prophecies. The concept of a global flood destroying civilization is not a new one. From the Epic of Gilgamesh recorded in twenty-seventh century B.C. Iraq through to Noah's Ark, stories of inundation are ingrained in the mythologies of numerous cultures around the world.

With rising sea levels being of concern to many as global warming sets in, it may very well be time to consider a world without glaciers. Although the chances of these ice-age relics disappearing completely in the foreseeable future is pretty remote, you just never know how things will turn out, especially when it comes to problems arising from humanity's collective stupidity.

Currently, about 10 percent of Earth's surface is covered with permanent ice. That adds up to about 7,200,000,000 cubic miles (30,000,000 km³) of ice amassed in the great icecaps of Antarctica and Greenland, the floating ice sheets of the Antarctic and ice packs of the Arctic, and permanent glaciers in the various mountains of the world.

It has been estimated that if all the permanent ice in the world were to melt, sea levels would rise by 230 ft. (70 m).

The amount of ice on Earth has varied significantly over the course of human history. During the height of the last ice age, around 18,000 years ago, ice sheets covered all of Canada and much of the American Northeast and Midwest, in some places reaching a thickness of 8,000–10,000 feet thick (2,400–3,000 m). Sea levels were as much as 130 meters (630 ft.) lower than they are today. At other times, sea levels have been significantly higher than at present.

It has been estimated that if all the permanent ice in the world were to melt, sea levels would rise by 230 ft. (70 m). As the expected temperature elevation through global warming may be anywhere between 36° F and 50° F (2° C and 10° C) over the next hundred years, and the average temperature of Antarctica is around -58° F (-50° C), there is little chance that all the glaciers are going to melt through predicted climate change alone. It's going to take something much more catastrophic than that. Even if they did melt, the rise in sea levels isn't nearly enough to cover the major landmasses.

However, when we couple the effects of elevated sea levels with the widespread and devastating impact of climate change in general, the effects would be significant. Crop failures, starvation, civil unrest, fresh water wars and whole nations of climate refugees on the move would be but the beginning of woes.

FOREWARNED IS FOREARMED

The exact nature of the apocalypse that awaits humanity will not be known until the doomsday. Although this presents us a considerable number of challenges, we must remain thankful that the Maya saw fit to warn us, at all, of the coming cataclysm.

Louis Pasteur said, "Chance favors the prepared mind." Acknowledging the reality of the forthcoming apocalypse is the first step toward taking the necessary action to protect yourself and your loved ones from doom. However, if we are to have any chance of surviving, we must utilize what little time we have left between now and December 21, 2012, to prepare ourselves both mentally and physically for any contingency.

What you do now to prepare for the coming cataclysm will determine how you can respond on the day it arrives. Your actions that day will determine whether you will have a personal future or will perish alongside the ill-prepared masses.

SECTION 4

D-DAY

"Let us eat and drink,
for tomorrow we die!"

—Isaiah 22:13

So, the big day has arrived at last. Like Noah before the deluge, you have fulfilled your moral duty to warn family, friends and neighbors of their imminent doom. You've finished boarding up your rural retreat or sealed the hatch on your backyard bunker. Your biohazard suit is neatly pressed and hanging by a wire coat hanger on the back of your barricaded door. You've put fresh batteries in your Geiger counter and checked that you've packed your *Seinfeld* box-set just one last time.

Now what?

You won't have long to wait. The apocalyptic dice has been rolled, and last bets have been placed.

However, no one can be sure just which way the cataclysmic pendulum will swing on D-Day. Within a few short hours, you will know whether your fastidious preparations and training have paid off. Will you receive the reward of survival and be welcomed with open arms into your own personal post-apocalyptic Valhalla, or will you join billions of other and die a swift but hideous death? There are no guarantees.

Because there are so many possible ways the world could end, it is well nigh impossible to be ready and waiting for each and every scenario on the day. You will need to make a choice between standing on a mountain top wearing the latest personal floatation device and scanning the horizon for breaking waves or hunkered down in your subterranean refuge, wearing your radiation suit and watching the needle on your trusty Geiger counter. You can't do both.

And if D-Day dawns to the hum of alien landing craft, you will know that you have bet on the wrong horseman of the apocalypse. At very least you may be able to say a quick "I told you so…" before you are blown to kingdom come by a laser canon.

Cowering in a basement, however, may not be how you want to greet the End of Days. You may be of the opinion that life in the post-apocalyptic world without your iPhone or Facebook account would not be worth living and would prefer to go out in a blaze of glory. On a night when there will be no morning after, you may want to toss caution to the four winds and damn the consequences, for there won't be any.

For those who have a will to survive, here are a few tips that may prove useful.

HOW TO SURVIVE AN ASTEROID IMPACT

Dateline: 7:14 A.M., June 30, 1908. The Tunguska River, Russia.

A small asteroid or comet fragment, less than 160 ft. (50 m) in diameter, entered the earth's atmosphere. It exploded some 3–6 miles (5–10 km) above the earth's surface, creating an airburst that flattened 830 square miles (2,150 km^2) of trees. It was estimated that the shockwave from the blast would have measured at least 5.0 on the Richter scale (the scale was not invented until 1935) and been equivalent to a 10–15 megaton bomb, or at very least 1,000 times as powerful as the atomic bomb dropped on Hiroshima.

The Tunguska Event, as it is known, is believed to have been the largest impact event in recent history. Capable of decimating vast metropolitan areas in seconds, impact events of this magnitude have happened all too frequently in Earth's past. Compared to some of the space rocks that have hit the earth, the Tunguska explosion was merely a popcorn burst. Imagine the devastation that could come from a 24-hour shower of these space pebbles. The only fragment of the Tunguska fragment believed to hit the earth

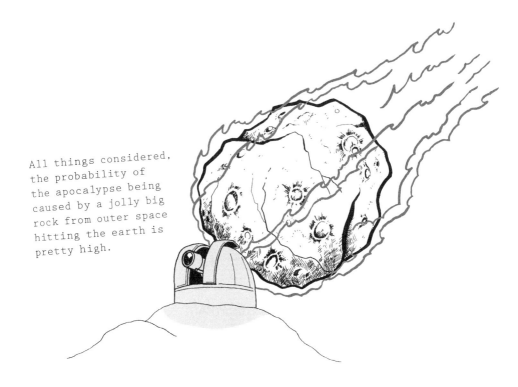

All things considered, the probability of the apocalypse being caused by a jolly big rock from outer space hitting the earth is pretty high.

created a 2,300 ft. (700 m) long crater, now Lake Cheko, and that fragment was only 3 ft. (1 m) in diameter.

All things considered, the probability of the apocalypse being caused by a jolly big rock from outer space hitting the earth is pretty high—high enough, at least, for the governments to spend millions on tracking Near-Earth Objects and developing contingency plans for dealing with rogue doomsday rocks. Significant impact events happen with a disquieting regularity, and it is reasonable to assume that at some point in humanity's future, we will have to deal with the aftermath of a collision. But do not abandon hope too soon. Survival is possible. If our primitive mammalian forebears could survive the asteroid impact that wiped out the dinosaurs 65 million years ago, how much more could we, as a species—with our unique ability to microwave pizzas and push all those tiny buttons on cell phones—survive another cataclysmic impact?

Don't Think It Can't Happen to You

That's exactly what the dinosaurs thought before their party was permanently pooped by a big rock falling out of the sky. Although it is highly improbable that you will ever be directly hit by a rock from outer space, it is not altogether impossible. There have been a number of reported incidents over the last century of people being hit by meteorites and surviving.

In June 2009, Gerrit Blank, a 14-year-old boy from Essen, Germany, was struck by a pea-sized meteorite as he walked to school. "At first I just saw a large ball of light and then I suddenly felt a pain in my hand," he told the media. "Then a split second after that there was an enormous bang like a crash of thunder. The noise that came after the flash of light was so loud that my ears were ringing for hours afterwards. When it hit me, it knocked me flying and then was still going fast enough to bury itself into the road."

The meteorite left a 0.3 in. (7 cm) long gash on the boy's hand. The red-hot rock was dug out of a 12 in. (30 cm) wide crater in the ground and sent to scientists who confirmed its extraterrestrial origin.

This was not the first time humans have ended up being targets in a celestial shooting gallery. The first recorded case in modern history of someone being struck by a meteorite occurred on November 30, 1954, in Sylacauga, Alabama, when Mrs. Elizabeth Hodges, asleep on her couch, was hit by a grapefruit-sized space rock that crashed through her roof, bounced off her radio and hit her on the upper leg, giving her a nasty bruise.

It is not, however, these trifling space stones that should concern us; it's their larger, much uglier brothers that will leave far more of an indelible impression.

On March 22, 1989, an asteroid larger than an aircraft carrier and four times the size of the object that devastated the Tunguska region in 1908, called 4581 Asclepius (also known as Apollo Asteroid 1989FC) missed the earth by an astronomical whisker. Traveling at a speed of more than 46,000 mph (74,000 kph), it missed us by a mere 400,000 miles (650,000 km), passing through the exact point in our orbit where we had been only six hours previously.

Had it struck the earth, the energy released would have been equivalent to a 2,500 megaton hydrogen bomb. That blast would excavate a crater 5–10 miles (8–16 km) in diameter within seconds, obliterating everything within a 40 mile (70 km) radius, and leaving an area the size of West Virginia totally devastated.

And why didn't our governments prepare the world for this possible doomsday asteroid? Despite the millions of dollars spent annually on discovering and tracking Near-Earth Objects, astronomers only discovered its existence eight days after this astronomical near miss.

4581 Asclepius is only one of thousands of Near-Earth Objects that could strike our planet without warning. In April 1990, a Congressional committee set up to assess the asteroid threat heard that objects the size of 4581 Asclepius probably whizzed past undetected once every two or three years.

Although the impact of 4581 Asclepius was not likely to have resulted in an Extinction Level Event, scientists have discovered more than 1,500 objects with diameters over 1,000 yards (1 km) that could have caused such total annihilation.

The one with our name on it is well overdue.

Watch the Skies

Although government agencies may try to conceal the existence of a doomsday asteroid to avoid mass panic, there is little they can do to stop amateur astronomers from spilling the beans about its existence. Some of the great astronomical discoveries of recent years have been made by backyard star gazers, with cups of coffee in one hand and eyes glued to the eyepieces of their homemade telescopes. Chances are, you'll find out about the upcoming end of humanity from some socially inept geek with a blog before you hear the emergency sirens start sounding.

Find a Subterranean Refuge

As simple as it may seem, the safest place to be during a doomsday asteroid impact is on the other side of the planet from where it hits. Unfortunately, the chances of you knowing where ground zero will be are pretty remote. The next best thing is to be underground, preferably deep underground.

Don't leave it to the last minute to start looking for a suitable subterranean shelter. You won't be the only one looking for a hole to crawl into. Secure some geological survey maps of your local area and look for natural cave formations or disused mines. Join a speleological society and clock some practical hours crawling through mud in the claustrophobic caverns of the underworld.

Don't leave it to the last minute to start looking for a
suitable subterranean shelter. You won't be the only one
looking for a hole to crawl into.

Even underground sewers and subways may offer you some
degree of protection if your area is pummelled by residual debris
from a passing comet. But there is little hope of survival if your
shelter sustains a direct hit overhead. At least you won't have to
worry about burial costs.

THINGS TO LOOK FOR WHEN CHOOSING AN UNDERGROUND HIDEOUT

Putting aside your fear of bats, spiders, bears, steaming
piles of guano, claustrophobia and the very rational threat
of being buried alive, caves are ideal for all those wanting to
keep a low profile on doomsday. While it is understandable

that many are apprehensive about the prospect of taking up residence in what is little more than a hole in the ground, the security that subterranean sanctuaries provide far outweigh the perils. With no conspicuous manmade structures to advertise your presence, caves offer the ultimate in "do not disturb" post-apocalyptic retreats. If it's good enough for NORAD, then it's good enough for you. Here are a few things to consider.

Off the Map

As most caves within easy reach of road access are known to speleologists, it may be difficult finding one without a queue waiting outside on doomsday. So make sure your cave is sufficiently off the map or difficult to access to deter other troglodytes. As GPS navigation systems will be out after the apocalypse, make sure you can find the cave entrance by map and compass alone. It may even help to practice finding it in the dark. Remember to thoroughly reconnoiter your cave before D-Day and hide your food, arms and survival gear where no one will find them.

Concealed Entrances

Ensure that all entrances to your cave are adequately concealed. Telltale footprints, broken twigs or overturned stones will soon lead unwelcome guests to your door. Utilize local vegetation and natural cover to disguise your presence.

Multiple Exits

The importance of multiple escape routes cannot be over-estimated. In the event that you are overrun by brigands, follow a tunnel to the surface. It may be a good idea to lay booby-traps that trigger a collapse upon your escape, to deter pursuit.

Water Supply

Water must flow in and, more importantly, flow out of your cave. Remember, all water should be filtered. At any one time, 30 percent of the earth's fresh water supplies can be found underground, so there's a good chance that, at very least, you will find a trickle somewhere.

A steadily flowing underground stream can also act as a sewage disposal system when heeding the call of nature outside is too dangerous. Ensure that there is no chance of backflow.

Air Flow

An adequate supply of fresh air is vital. Toxic gases can quickly build up in caves or mine tunnels that are inade-quately ventilated. Ensure that cooking fires are located near a suitable air outflow point. Remember to only light your fires at night to reduce the possibility of roving brigands locating your hideout by smoke trail.

Storm Water

Look for high water marks in your cave before taking up residence. What may appear to be a safe haven from the celestial firestorm may become a raging torrent after rainfall.

Extreme Makeover

The harsh reality of living in a cave will not take long to sink in; the cold, dank darkness; the incessant dripping of water; the shrill cry of bats, like fingernails on a chalkboard. What will initially be somewhat of an adventure will soon threaten to throw you into the pits of despair unless a few simple measures are taken to make your hole into a home. Bearing in mind the limitations of your situation, your renovations need not be elaborate. Your efforts may not result in you adorning the cover of the next issue of *Better Caves and Sewers*, but it could, at least, bring some degree of cheer to an otherwise dingy dugout.

Cave envy is a thing of the past. There is no more keeping up with the Joneses, as there are no more Joneses. You are now free to live exactly how you want to live.

Even the most depressing rock walls can be brightened up with a splash of paint. Mankind has been decorating cave walls with painting and petroglyphs for millennia. Begin by trying a few simple hand stencils before moving on to more technically challenging artistic expressions. Like the cave dwellers of old, who painted such cultural icons of their day as mammoth and bison, you too can commemorate the glory

What will initially be somewhat of an adventure will soon threaten to throw you into the pits of despair unless a few simple measures are taken to make your hole into a home.

days of western civilization with renditions of the humble cell phone, the pop-up toaster and the AK-47 assault rifle.

Building permits: a thing of the past. After dabbling with a bit decorating, you can go wild with the renovations. Transform that annoying trickle of water along the cave floor into an in-ground spa. Adding an extra playroom for the kids is as simple as a few back-breaking months with a pick and shovel. The possibilities are endless.

Prepare For the Long Haul

While the impact of a 1,000 ft. (300 m) space rock would not bring about doomsday all by itself, it serves to remind us of the devastation that even a relatively small piece of celestial debris can cause. There is no doubt that an impact in your neighborhood would ruin your day, but globally the effect would be minimal.

An Extinction Level Event brought about by the impact of a 1,000 yard (1 km) object would, however, bring the post-apocalyptic world of the Hollywood blockbuster from the big screen to your back door. Even if you were to survive the impact and global firestorm, you'd have years of frigid, ash-covered twilight to worry about. Oh, and cannibals. Maybe being at ground zero might not be as bad as it sounds. At least you'll go out with a bang.

HOW TO SURVIVE A MEGA-TSUNAMI

If the tsunamis of recent years are anything to go by, then you may have a lot more to worry about than getting a parking spot or a touch of sunburn if you choose to spend your final day at the seaside. The Boxing Day tsunami of 2004, responsible for killing over 230,000 people, was no more than a ripple in a teacup compared to some waves that have swept across our oceans in the past.

The largest wave ever recorded was in the early hours of July 9, 1958 in Lituya Bay, Alaska. Following an earthquake registering almost 8 on the Richter scale, a mountainside collapsed into the headwaters of a narrow fiord. The resulting wave reached a maximum height of 1,720 ft. (524 m). That's 266 ft. (81 m) higher than the top of the lighting rod on the Empire State Building (1,454 ft. /

443m). By comparison, the Boxing Day tsunami reached a peak of possibly 100 ft. (30 m) in some places but was generally less than 30 ft. (10 m) high. Three fishing boats were on Lituya Bay at the time. One sank with the loss of two lives, while two others managed to ride the wave to safety, with four survivors.

Unlike normal tsunamis, which are generally produced from tectonic activity or the sudden raising or lowering of the seabed, these mega-tsunamis are produced by large-scale landslides or significant impact events, such as an asteroid hitting the earth. A general rule of thumb is that the larger the rock to hit the pond, the bigger the wave. With boulders the size of Rhode Island crossing Earth's orbital path from time to time, you may need more than a pair of floaties to survive the ripples one of these puppies makes. Consider the following tips.

Head for the Hills

Mega-tsunamis could travel at least 20 miles (30 km) or more inland depending on the local topography and the size of the wave. To be safe, you need to be as far away from the coast as possible, preferably in an elevated position. Don't leave your evacuation to the last moment. When the sirens start sounding, it will be too late. Every man and his dog will be throwing a box of valuables into the back of the sedan and hitting the road. There will be little chance of you getting clear in time even if the roads were empty, let alone gridlocked with horn-sounding motorists fleeing an imminent dunking. Remember, waves can wash further up a slope than their actual crest height.

To be safe from mega-tsunamis, you need to be as far away from the coast as possible, preferably in an elevated position. Don't leave your evacuation to the last moment.

Forget About Putting on Your Running Shoes

In the open ocean, tsunamis can travel as fast as a jumbo jet (600 mph or 965 kph). Although their speed slows significantly in shallow waters near the coast, by the time you see one, it will be too late. Sounding like a freight train from hell, the best you can hope for are a few moments to make your peace with your chosen deity.

Watch for Sudden Exposure of the Seafloor

Tsunamis may sometimes be preceded by what is known as a drawdown, where the ocean suddenly recedes, leaving hapless beachgoers walking on the exposed shallow sea floor pointing at flapping fish. This is caused by the trough (lowest part of the wave between the crests) of the wave reaching the shore before the crest. Be warned: Drawdowns do not always happen; sometimes you'll have no warning. The first thing you'll see, and quite possibly the last thing you'll ever see, will be a foaming tower of death breaking over your picnic.

Stay Afloat

If worse comes to worst and you find yourself swept away in one of these washing machines from hell, try to make your way to the surface as quickly as possible. Apart from drowning, most deaths during a tsunami result from injuries sustained from being pummelled by submerged debris. Claw your way to the surface and drag yourself onto anything afloat; the bigger the better.

Claw your way to the surface and drag yourself onto anything afloat; the bigger the better.

> **SHIPS AHOY!**
>
> The safest place to be when confronted by a tsunami is out to sea. In deep ocean water, a tsunami forms only a small, harmless swell, generally less than 3 feet (1 m) in height; most of the power of the tsunami is deep beneath the surface. It is only as it approaches the shallow waters of a coastline that it grows into the vertical wall of death so often portrayed in disaster films. In the open ocean, tsunamis are barely distinguishable from normal, wind-generated waves and will often go unnoticed by seafarers.
>
> Now is the time to join a yacht club or make a friend at the local marina. Take a course in open-water boat handling skills and be prepared to commandeer a vessel if the need arises. Lifejackets are essential.

Watch Out for Wave Sets

Just like ripples on a pond, tsunamis come in sets of three or more waves. The first may not necessarily be the largest. Surviving the first wave does not guarantee you are out of danger. Use the time between the arrival of each wave to further secure your position or move to higher ground.

Seek Refuge

Avoid inundated areas for at least twenty-four hours. Travel through disaster areas after this time should be restricted to avoid hindering rescue services, looters and civil unrest. If not already positioned in a secure location, head inland via back roads or waterways. Remember, the days immediately after the apocalypse will be the most hazardous, as survivors realize their predicament and try to take advantage of others' preparations.

HOW TO SURVIVE A SOLAR STORM

Just before midday on September 1, 1859, the eminent British astronomer Richard Carrington observed an enormous solar flare on the surface of the sun. Erupting from a sunspot aimed directly at the earth, a massive cloud of magnetically charged plasma, called a coronal mass ejection (CME), swept 91 million miles (146 million km) between the sun and our planet in less than eighteen hours (it usually takes three or four days).

As the supercharged particles washed over our planet, they created the largest geomagnetic storm in recorded history. Skies around the globe erupted in spectacular displays of red, purple and green auroras, so bright in some places that newspapers could be read at midnight. Auroras, usually only seen at the poles, were even visible from tropical latitudes over such places as Hawaii and the Caribbean.

Most alarming was the solar storm's impact on the only technology vulnerable to power surges at the time. The telegraph system was disrupted worldwide, with some telegraph operators being shocked by electrical discharges and, in some cases, telegraph paper bursting into flames.

Since then, solar flares have periodically knocked out regional communication and electricity grids around the world. Although

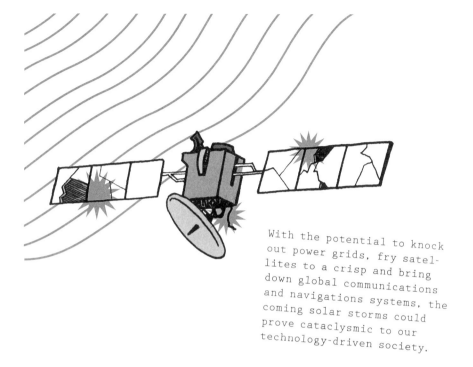

With the potential to knock out power grids, fry satellites to a crisp and bring down global communications and navigations systems, the coming solar storms could prove cataclysmic to our technology-driven society.

what is now known as the Carrington Event is the largest geomagnetic storm in more than five hundred years, scientists cannot rule out that storms of a similar magnitude or even larger could occur within the next few years.

Damage from the 1859 solar storms was not great. But as our modern society is so heavily dependent on technology, our way of life is now significantly more vulnerable to solar activity.

In an uncanny coincidence, 2012 marks the peak of the sun's eleven-year solar cycle that scientists at the National Center for Atmospheric Research (NCAR) have predicted could be the most intense solar maximum in 50 years.

With the potential to knock out power grids, fry satellites to a crisp and bring down global communications and navigations systems, the coming solar storms could prove cataclysmic to our technology-driven society. We would effectively be turning back our lifestyle clock by one hundred years. Imagine the aftermath of Hurricane Katrina, worldwide, for months or even years. With no banking, electric gas pumps, oil refineries, transportation, refrigeration, news reports, sewage disposal, tap water, phone services, Internet or supermarket grocery shopping, how long would it be before all hell broke loose on the streets? Three days without power and the natives get restless; three weeks and it's *Lord of the Flies* all over again. It may be time to start battening the hatches.

Here are a few things to consider.

Three days without power and the natives get restless; three weeks and it's *Lord of the Flies* all over again.

Look for Pretty Lights

The pretty lights in the night sky may not exactly be the apocalypse most people will be thinking of, but they could herald a U-turn for western civilization. Aurora displays around the equator are a sure sign to pack your bags and phone a friend on a commune. If nature were to press the "off button" on our electricity-dependent lifestyles, then we are only days away from Darwin's survival of the fittest.

Living without electricity is no novelty to over 1.6 billion people living in the world today. But for us in first world countries, the impact on society would be monumental. It is imperative that you have your evacuation plan in place well before doomsday and are ready to implement it at a moment's notice. Anarchy has a very short fuse.

Take the Long and Winding Road

The last place you want to be when the power switch goes off is in the cities; the greater the concentration of humanity, the greater the trouble. Allow the tyranny of distance to work in your favor; establish a well-stocked retreat as far from the madding crowds as possible. Of course, your retreat must be completely self-sustaining—capable of providing your every need. There will be no more popping down to the corner store to pick up a carton of milk. The only milk you will ever get again will be squeezed by your own hand. But do you know how to make butter? How about making a bar of soap or a candle from scratch? Can you grow your own food, grind grain or skin an animal? Can you make antibiotics, prescription lenses or extract teeth? Can you imagine a world without toilet paper? Think about it. Maybe living in community doesn't sound too bad after all. But then, you must choose your living companions very wisely.

All that is ahead of you. Surviving D-Day is the easy part. The days that follow are what you really have to worry about.

HOW TO SURVIVE A ROBOT INSURRECTION

Short of robot hordes inundating the earth through a time portal from the future, or sweeping down from the mothership in a coordinated invasion from outer space, there is little possibility in the next few years of robotic technologies being developed to the stage where they could actually revolt against their human overlords. But you can never be too careful with machines. Even if your witless domestic appliances were to stage a revolution, things could get very nasty indeed. It doesn't take much imagination to think of what could happen if the lawn mower, kitchen blender or even your humble toaster was bent on evil.

In the event that you do wake on D-Day to the sound of nano-robots scuttling across your floor or cars on the street being crushed by an armor-plated, laser-toting, 50-ft.-high megabot, here are a few things to remember.

Remember That Robots Are Not Evil

It is not malice you see in the ember red photoreceptors of the robot about to squeeze the life from your writhing body; it is the cold stare of indifference. Robots are not evil. They are only as bad as the minds that create them. Don't take their attempts to kill you personally. Robots are just doing what they were pro-grammed to do. In and of themselves, they are no more villainous than your average electric toothbrush. Left to their own devices, robots are much more content sitting around contemplating how to apply the Navier-Stokes Equation to brewing the perfect cup of tea, than goosestepping en masse and laser-blasting their way to world domination.

Yet, it is important we don't forget that the robots you are most likely to encounter on doomsday will not have heard of, let alone been programmed to follow, Asimov's Three Laws of Robotics, so don't expect them to play fair.

Neither must we afford robots the courtesy of human rights, as even the most humanoid of robots is not human. So take off the proverbial gloves and feel free to do whatever it takes to get the job done. Decommission each unit with extreme prejudice and sleep the sleep of the righteous that night.

Build Up Your Running Speed

Robots are formidable adversaries. Basically, if you are within range of their sensors, they will find you and hunt you down like the animal you are. Apart from possessing motion-sensing and thermal-imaging receptors, robots may have a startling array of high-tech sensors, including very acute sound perception. Your best chance, if unprepared to confront your metallic nemeses, is to put as much distance between yourself and their long-range weaponry as possible. Feel no shame at making a hasty tactical retreat if the situation warrants it. He who turns and runs away lives to fight another day.

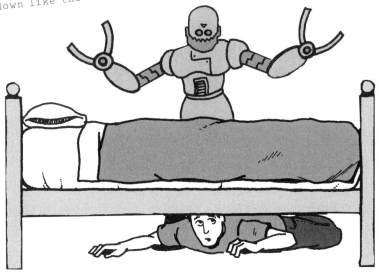

If you are within range of robots' sensors, they will find you and hunt you down like the animal you are.

Pull the Plug

There's more than one way to deactivate a rampaging robot. The method that you employ will depend on a number of factors, including what weapons you have at hand, your physical and mental condition, the environment you find yourself in and the type of robot that is trying to kill you.

Whenever possible, try to take out a robot from a distance. The closer you are to a robot, the greater the danger you are in. If your endeavors to thwart its relentless advance fail, run first, and then try and improve your strategic position before attempting another strike.

Wire cutters and tin snips are useful weapons during close-quarter combat. Sever as many exposed wires or tubes as you can.

Most robots are not thermonuclear, so it doesn't matter which color you cut first.

Attempts to bludgeon a robot into submission will usually prove futile. A robot's armor-plated body is impervious to all but the most well-placed blows. If you are cornered or find yourself in a hand-to-hand combat situation, a few strategic strikes to its vulnerable visual receptors can render a robot momentarily confused. Once blinded, you can either make your escape or invest a few extra moments to decommission it completely.

If worse comes to worst and you find yourself with a robot's cold, metal fingers locked in a vice-like grip around your neck, try to find its "off" switch. As surprising as it may seem, the simplest solutions are often the most effective.

Bear in mind that a power switch can sometimes be difficult to locate in the heat of the battle. It usually can be found beneath a

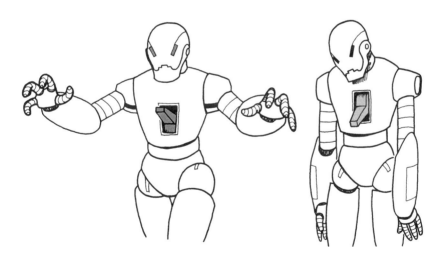

If worse comes to worst and you find yourself with a robot's cold, metal fingers locked in a vice-like grip around your neck, try to find its "off" switch.

concealed panel somewhere on the robot's back or head. Powering down may only take a few seconds; extracting yourself from its frozen grip may take considerably longer.

If time and resources permit, hunt down the universal off switch that will deactivate the entire robot army. Usually located at some seemingly impenetrable central control facility, the switch or button, as the case may be, will be heavily defended. Although the chances of success are slim, the glory in victory will be substantial.

THE THREE LAWS OF ROBOTICS

The Three Laws of Robotics were written by acclaimed science fiction writer Isaac Asimov. They are a set of rules hardwired into almost all the robots appearing his fictional work. The key point here is that they are fiction. Don't expect the robots you encounter on D-Day to demonstrate such social niceties. The rules are, as follows:

A robot may not injure a human being or, through inaction, allow a human being to come to harm.

A robot must obey any orders given to it by human beings, except where such orders would conflict with the First Law.

A robot must protect its own existence as long as such protection does not conflict with the First or Second Law.

HOW TO SURVIVE A ZOMBIE APOCALYPSE

If you put your ear to bunker doors across the nation in the quiet before the dawn of December 21, 2012, you will hear a fervent mantra whispered by many diehard survivalists as they polish the barrels of their pump-action shotguns just one last time.

"Please let there be zombies. Please let there be zombies."

Since their first appearance in modern form in George A. Romero's 1978 film *Dawn of the Dead*, zombies have eaten their way into our hearts and minds to become pop culture icons.

Dismiss zombies from the doomsday equation at your peril. If life teaches us anything, it is that you should expect the unexpected. And as there are few apocalypse scenarios more unexpected than zombies, this may be the one to place your bets on, even at astronomical odds. It would be a fool indeed who does not, at very least, have a contingency plan in place to deal with an undead world. Heaven help those who sneer at the thought of a zombie apocalypse, for they will invariably be the first ones clasping their entrails as they try and drag themselves away from a ravenous horde of living dead on Z-Day.

Don't say you haven't been warned.

There are a few things that you probably need to know to avoid becoming a mobile Happy Meal.

Don't Panic

Of all the possible apocalypse scenarios, zombies are, at least initially, one of the least dramatic. The chances of you actually seeing a zombie on D-Day is quite remote. The most you would be likely see is the tail-end of a television news report of a bizarre murder somewhere in the Alaskan tundra or an SMS from a friend directing you to some shaky YouTube cell phone footage that "just has to be a hoax." But don't let the lack of fanfare fool you. A zombie apocalypse may have a slow start, but it will soon snowball into a gorefest that will leave the majority of humanity as walking leftovers in just a few short weeks.

While the first media broadcasts of people being eaten alive in the streets will be greeted with skeptical disbelief by most, consider it a sign to immediately implement your survival plan. Time is still on your side. You have up to twenty-four hours in which to escape to your rural retreat or mountain refuge before the roads from the cities are choked with those fleeing the undead hordes.

Although it will, at times, be difficult to believe a zombie apocalypse is actually happening, the sooner you accept the reality of the situation, the greater your chances of survival. You may not be at ground zero on Z-Day, but how you react on the first day will determine if you still have all your body parts by the end of the week.

Know Your Enemy

It is impossible to know the exact nature of the zombie threat prior to the apocalypse. But one thing is for sure: They won't be running. Popular though the fast so-called zombies of recent celluloid features may be, real zombies are slow. Think about it. Death is the ultimate inhibitor. If one comes back from death, one is hardly likely to be imbued with superpowers. You would be a mere shadow of your former self. Zombies shamble, shuffle and stagger; they don't sprint, vault over abandoned cars or launch choreographed attacks that look more like the New York City Marathon.

One thing is for sure: They won't be running. Popular though the fast so-called zombies of recent celluloid features may be, real zombies are slow.

You can easily sidestep a zombie. Run rings around one if you like. But it's the moment that you become overconfident and let down your guard that you will feel the shattered teeth of some legless ghoul latching onto your ankle.

Zombies should never be underestimated. They are relentless, merciless and almost unstoppable.

Pick Them Off From a Distance

Projectile weapons, such as bows and arrows, guns, RPGs and even nuclear missiles were invented for a reason: to put as much distance between you and your adversary as possible, while still inflicting a mortal wound. The closer you are to your enemy, the greater the chance that they can inflict an injury on you. Close-order combat

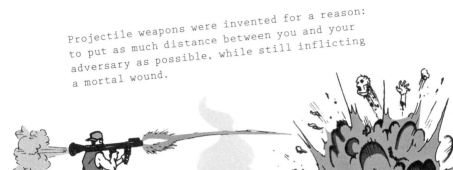

Projectile weapons were invented for a reason: to put as much distance between you and your adversary as possible, while still inflicting a mortal wound.

with zombies should only be engaged in as a last resort; it poses significant risks to your safety. But sometimes, there will simply be no avoiding it. You will just have to get your hands dirty.

Although an assortment of handheld weapons have been used with spectacular results in many Hollywood movies, in reality, using bludgeons, such as baseball bats and gardening tools, is fraught with potential dangers and should only be considered when there are no other options.

A zombie does not need to take a bite out your left arm to contaminate you. The facts are that the zombie virus is transmitted through body fluids. Anybody slicing a zombie in two with a chainsaw or impaling one with a fence post is likely to be drenched in infected gore. It only takes one drop of blood or other body fluids for you to join the legion of undead.

Even with a handgun, the chances of you hitting a small, moving target, such as a zombie's head, is very low. At close range (less than three yards), trained professionals, such as police officers, have less than a forty percent chance of hitting their target in a field situation.

Play it safe. Pick them off from a distance.

Keep Quiet

Noise attracts zombies. Need I say more?

Wear Protective Clothing

That small scratch on the back of your hand you got while foraging for food in a dimly lit supermarket but never got round to putting a bandaid on could be more of a threat to what's left of your life than you may first think. You don't have to have your left leg unexpectedly gnawed off by a zombie postal worker to become infected. Any cut or abrasion can be an access point for infection. Also, screaming for divine assistance as you plunge your 11-in. Stanley screwdriver into a zombie's vacant eye socket may not be as good an idea as it seems at the time. Infected blood or brain tissue spraying into your open mouth or eyes could see you joining the ranks of the undead before the weekend.

It is of vital importance that you be appropriately attired before engaging in any melee with the living dead. This includes full face protection, such as a handyman's face shield or goggles and a surgical mask. Although you may look more like an abattoir worker than a hired assassin, at least you won't have to worry about waking up to find yourself dead the next morning.

Never Turn Your Back

It goes without saying that you can never assume a zombie is "dead" just because it is down for the count. Zombies have a nasty habit of lurching to their feet again when you least expect it, even if you have pumped a couple of quick rounds into their cranium. Bullets are strange things and can often be harmlessly deflected by skull bone, leaving a zombie's grey matter fully intact.

Zombies have the remarkable ability to keep going despite dropping body parts like the leaves of autumn. It is prudent to give even fully dismembered zombies (think, Black Knight from *Monty Python and the Holy Grail*) a wide berth, as they are sometimes capable of rolling like tumble weeds to savage their prey.

Also, bear in mind that, in certain situations, it can be quite difficult to distinguish between the living and the living dead. Those dearly departed, who have not long joined the ranks of the undead, may display few outward signs of decomposition. You cannot assume that the awkward gait and gormless expression on the face of the guy from apartment 101 means that he is a zombie. If in doubt, take evasive action.

Aim For the Head

When it comes to zombies, anything less than a head shot is a waste of valuable time and effort. Dispense with your classic "two to the center mass, one to the head" routine. "Double taps" or "hammered pairs" to the head are what counts; anything else is just window dressing.

When it comes to zombies, anything less than a head shot is a waste of valuable time and effort.

Overcome Your Squeamishness

The post-apocalyptic world of the undead is not for the squeamish. The sooner you overcome your natural aversion blood and guts, the sooner you will be able to take the new world order in your stride and carve a niche for yourself.

HOW TO SURVIVE AN ALIEN INVASION

On October 8, 1955, General Douglas Macarthur is reputed to have said, "The nations of the world will have to unite, for the next war will be an interplanetary war. The nations of the earth must someday make a common front against attack by people from other planets." While the thought of this alien invasion may not be utmost in your mind as you make your preparations for doomsday, it would be dangerously remiss not to at least consider the possibility.

An alien invasion on D-Day will certainly be a ball from far left field. That, no doubt, is all part of their nefarious plan. Aliens know their stuff. They have been conducting surveillance operations on Earth for many centuries and are fully aware of not only our military capabilities but also our general disbelief in their existence. They know our weak spots and will exploit them without hesitation. We can expect an attack to be swift and without mercy.

Nobody wants to wake on doomsday to the hum of alien landing craft and the embarrassing realization that they know nothing about alien death rays or force fields. Although the challenge of preparing for an attack from an adversary whose military capabilities, or dietary habits for that matter, are unknown, there are a few things we can do to avoid being caught with our metaphorical pants down.

Stay Out of Sight

It's reasonable to assume that when they come, they will come with all guns blazing. Death rays and other directed energy weapons, long portrayed in science fiction, should never be underestimated. However, even when wielded by gifted tentacles, they are not necessarily a death sentence. Avoiding being sliced in two can be as simple as staying out of the alien gunship's line of sight. Although ray guns can be fired from incredible distances with pinpoint accuracy, they can't fire around corners. Bear in mind that near-hits can still shower you with shrapnel and other flying debris.

Although ray guns can be fired from incredible distances with pinpoint accuracy, they can't fire around corners.

Get Away: The Farther the Better

We all know that it only takes one blast from a heat ray to blow your home to kingdom come, so there is little point sandbagging the front porch. Domestic, commercial and industrial centers will be the focus of their initial attack, followed by mop-up operations in regional areas. Backcountry cabins and remote rural homesteads will provide sanctuary in the short term, but be prepared to abandon these at a moment's notice.

Tune Up Your Bicycle

Alien invaders are most likely to use some form of electromagnetic pulse weapon to take out our technological infrastructure prior to their assault. Electromagnetic pulses, or EMPs, create a power surge that effectively fry all unprotected electrical equipment, global communications networks and even entire power grids within seconds. As these EMPs can permanently immobilize vehicles with electronic ignitions and control systems, don't expect to be able to jump into your SUV to escape the mayhem. Unless you've pre-empted the rush, you and literally millions of others will be fleeing on foot from the major urban centers. Now is the time to pump the tires of your bike and do a bit of training.

Avoid Your Neighbor

There will be no safety in numbers during an alien invasion. In fact, quite the opposite is true. Large assemblies of people are more likely to attract the attention of our alien foe. Using minor roads or even waterways increases your chances of escaping unscathed. Also, your biggest threat, apart from the aliens, will be from your fellow refugees.

Dig In

Subterranean caverns such as caves or old mine shafts make ideal refuges from extraterrestrial invaders. They not only provide concealment from their sophisticated scanning devices, but also protection from death rays and other forms of alien weaponry. They also provide a base from which your future guerrilla campaign can be launched.

Those who choose to remain in urban areas can utilize subways and underground drainage and sewage systems for shelter. Don't wait until the invasion begins to locate these underground facilities. Secure maps from local government agencies showing manhole covers or other entry points and make sure you have the necessary

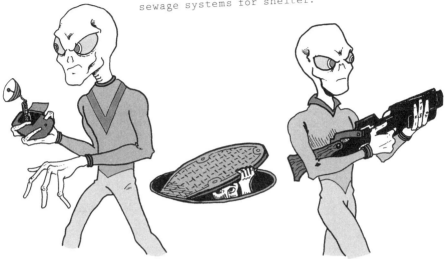

Those who choose to remain in urban areas can utilize subways and underground drainage and sewage systems for shelter.

tools to access them. Remember, other people competing for space in these prized sanctuaries may be more of a threat to your safety the laser-toting aliens on the surface.

JUST THE BEGINNING

So, you've survived D-Day. Well done! Chalk number one up on your bunker wall. Don't give yourself a self-congratulatory pat on the back too soon though. This is but the beginning of woes. The weeping and gnashing of teeth comes a little later.

Depending on the type of doomsday you have just survived, you could be facing any number of possible post-apocalyptic worlds—each with their own specific survival criteria. Your ability to be the last man/woman standing will depend solely on your adaptability and personal resolve.

We are not, however, a ship without a rudder on the post-apocalyptic high seas. Many have set sail through the world of the undead/nuclear wasteland/machine domination/etc. before. Well, maybe not literally, but through the viaducts of their minds. Hollywood has presented us with a veritable smorgasbord of doomsday advice from decades of post-Armageddon films. Let the wise take heed. Let no one say that they haven't been warned.

SECTION 5

ALTERNATE ENDINGS

"Today is a good day to die."
—Crazy Horse

A journey of a thousand miles starts with the first step. Your first step was surviving D-Day. That was the easy part. The days that follow will determine if you have what it takes to prevail in the global End of Days theme park. Although the exact nature of the apocalypse to befall humanity will remain a mystery until the bitter end, we are not totally in the dark about how life will be in the new and foreboding world that follows. There are many lessons that can be learned prior to the big day by a study of the diverse cinematic representations of the post-apocalyptic world. What better way to prepare for the coming apocalypse than by sitting in the comfort of your own home and reviewing the doomsday films of the last fifty years? Any knowledge that you gain vicariously now can only reduce the severity of your learning curve after Armageddon.

And who better to act as role models than our Hollywood heroes? If we can survive only half of the trouble they get themselves into on the big screen, then we are pretty well assured of surviving all that the post-apocalyptic world can throw at us. You just never know when asking yourself, "What would Bruce Willis do?" may be the difference between life and hideous death.

NUCLEAR WASTELAND

> "We are gonna survive this."
> —THE MAN FROM *THE ROAD*

Of all the potential post-apocalyptic worlds we could inherit, the ashen wastelands of a nuclear aftermath pose maybe the most serious threats to your long-term survival.

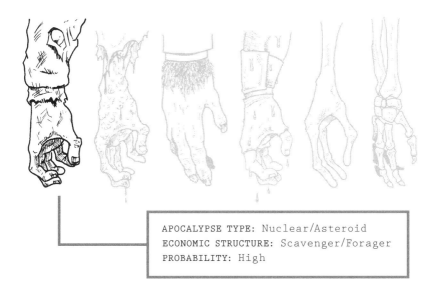

```
APOCALYPSE TYPE: Nuclear/Asteroid
ECONOMIC STRUCTURE: Scavenger/Forager
PROBABILITY: High
```

While even a small-scale regional strike of a hundred nuclear bombs may kill anywhere between 3 and 16 million people, depending on the target areas, the global impact of 1 to 5 million tons of smoke rising into the upper atmosphere and subsequent mini-ice-age could potentially kill billions. With limited food production and distribution from anywhere between five to ten years, most of the world's population would die of starvation.

With over eight thousand active nuclear warheads in the world today (and more than 23,000 in total), it's clear that the *a* in apocalypse may very well stand for atomic.

Although the situation will be grim, do not abandon hope just yet. Where there's a will, there's a way.

Case Study: *The Road* (2009)

This film, directed by John Hillcoat and starring Viggo Mortensen, is based on the 2006 novel of the same name by Cormac McCarthy and traces a father and son's harrowing journey through the post-apocalyptic wastelands of North America. Pushing a shopping cart of meager possessions, the dishevelled pair trudge through an endless, ash-covered landscape towards the sea, where they hope to find sanctuary. With little more than personal resolve to survive and a pistol with a single bullet, they face the constant threat from ruthless brigands and marauding cannibals.

Although the cataclysmic events that befell the world are unmentioned in the film, they bear all the hallmarks of either a nuclear holocaust, asteroid impact, supervolcano eruption or some other global environmental catastrophe. For the purpose of this study, we will consider the first of these scenarios. This is the post-apocalyptic world at its very worst.

Other Movies to Study: *The Postman* (1997), *Mad Max: Beyond Thunderdome* (1985)

RULES OF SURVIVAL: NUCLEAR WASTELAND

Stay Indoors

During a nuclear surface blast, millions of tons of earth are vaporized and lifted high into the atmosphere in a giant mushroom cloud. Dust contaminated with radioactive atoms is dispersed by the wind and eventually falls back to Earth. Each contaminated particle in this fallout acts like a miniature X-ray machine giving off invisible radiation capable of causing sickness or death after prolonged exposure.

Fortunately, the danger from this radioactive fallout lessens quickly over time. Many of the radioactive isotopes used in nuclear bombs are relatively short-lived; natural radioactive decay results in a dramatic decrease in the danger within hours of a detonation. Even though fallout may remain radioactive for months and spread tens of thousands of kilometers around the globe, much of it may not be any more hazardous than the radiation you are typically exposed to from domestic appliances, such as your TV set.

Unless you experience heavy fallout directly downwind from a nuclear strike zone, you need only shelter in your bunker for a few weeks. After this time, radiation will probably have dropped to levels that will allow you to spend an increasing number of hours outside each day. Limited exposure is not something to be overly concerned about. The human body has the capacity to repair most low-level radiation damage, leaving no long-term side effects. Extreme exposure will, however, cause sickness and death within days. Those who do survive after high-level exposure may face cancer, cataract formation, radio-dermatitis, decreased fertility and genetic mutations.

Because ionizing radiation is undetectable to your senses, and the damage it causes to the body is cumulative and related to the total dosage received, check your exposure levels with a dosimeter to be on the safe side.

Bundle Up

The indirect effects of a global nuclear war would have devastating consequences for the planet. Smoke from burning cities would be lofted by solar heating into the upper atmosphere, where it would remain for years, creating a blanket over the earth preventing solar heat from reaching the ground and producing a climate change unprecedented in recorded human history.

Some climate models have projected that average global surface temperatures would plummet by about 45° F (7° C). Make sure you pack your long johns and a warm coat.

Some climate models have projected that average global surface temperatures would plummet by about 45° F (7° C). When we consider that global average cooling during the last ice age 18,000 years ago was only around 41° F (5° C), we can begin to see the implications for humanity. With the largest temperature changes occurring over land, we could expect cooling of more than 68° F (20° C) over North America and 86° F (30° C) over much of Eurasia, with global precipitation falling by almost half. Agriculture would be impossible for at least a decade. Most people, except those with an adventurous palette, will starve to death.

Make sure you pack your long johns and a warm coat.

Avoid UV Rays

Studies have shown that even a limited nuclear exchange involving a hundred or so Hiroshima-sized nuclear devices between, for example, India and Pakistan, would produce massive urban fires, pumping more than 5 million metric tons of soot about 50 miles (80 km) into the stratosphere. This soot would absorb enough solar radiation to heat the surrounding gases, resulting in a series of chemical reactions that would break down the ozone layer that protects the earth from dangerous ultraviolet radiation.

More than 20 percent of the ozone layer would be lost globally, with more than 25–45 percent lost at mid-latitudes and up to 70 percent in higher latitudes.

There would be a significant increase in skin cancer and cataracts in those people scratching for food in the ash-covered wastelands. It would be wise to cover any exposed skin when making forays into the open from your bunker.

Not only would this increase in harmful UV light damage plants and animals in natural ecosystems, it would also result in a significant increase in skin cancer and cataracts in those people scratching for food in the ash-covered wastelands.

It would be wise to cover any exposed skin when making forays into the open from your bunker. Although you'll most likely already be wearing winter clothing to protect you from the cold, it is also important to don a broad-brimmed hat, gloves and sunglasses.

MUTANT MAYHEM

Although studies carried out on children conceived by parents exposed to radiation during World War II revealed no greater incidence of genetic abnormalities than the children born to unexposed parents, it always pays to err on the side of caution.

Unlike zombies, mutants are unpredictable. With such a staggering number of genetic anomalies possible, you just never know what sort of mutant you are going to encounter. Whether it be a hideous disfigurement or unapparent superhuman ability, you must always expect the unexpected.

It is important that when you encounter a mutant for the first time that you are not distracted by its grotesque deformities. The moment lost in saying "What the... ," may be all it needs to gain the upper hand in a tight situation. Mutants have also been known to play the sympathy card before turning on their politically correct prey in a frenzied

---

knife attack or worse. He who hesitates is lost. Do-gooders will be the first to bite the dust in the post-apocalyptic world.

Movies to Study: *The Hills Have Eyes* (1977), *The Island of Dr. Moreau* (1977), *Wrong Turn* (2003).

Watch Out for Cannibals

Although a distasteful subject for many, cannibalism is not a topic that should be swept neatly under the post-apocalyptic carpet. Although long stigmatized in polite circles as the epitome of barbarism, when social niceties are cast to the four winds, you may very well find yourself in the proverbial stew if you fail to take some simple precautions. Here are a few things to keep in mind.

WASTE NOT, WANT NOT

The "offal" truth of the matter is that people will, on occasion, eat other people. As unpalatable as this may seem, we must prepare ourselves for each and every contingency if we are to remain at the top of the post-apocalyptic food chain, and not end up as nothing more than a mobile delicatessen.

For the purposes of your survival, it is important that we distinguish between the two fundamental types of cannibal: Those who are cannibals due to hunger and those who are trying to make a philosophical statement. The former, although possibly highly motivated, may be easier to deal with than the latter.

Humanity has a long and ignoble history of eating other sentient creatures on our planet. In fact, there are few things off

If the psychological and cultural inhibitions we have for eating our neighbors are overcome, then everyone you pass on the street becomes a veritable fast-food outlet.

limits to the adventurous gastronaut. Yet, in today's society, the line seems to be firmly drawn at members of our own species. If the psychological and cultural inhibitions we have for eating our neighbors are overcome, then everyone you pass on the street becomes a veritable fast-food outlet.

In a time of post-nuclear famine, not everyone can afford the luxury of being picky when it comes to their dietary habits. When faced with sifting through ash-covered fields for beetle larvae or the odd wizened root, species prejudice may soon wear a little thin and a freshly carved and marinaded human round steak, served with a zesty roadside salad, may start to look a little more appealing. It is important to remember that most cannibals are people just like you, only they have a different culinary ethic.

If cannibals of necessity are a bit hard to stomach, then you may definitely have bitten off more than you can chew if you meet a cannibal of ideology. Although much rarer, those who are cannibals by philosophical choice can present a formidable obstacle to keeping all your bits and pieces firmly intact. What better way of demonstrating your dominance over your enemy than eating them? It represents the highest vindication of Darwin's "survival of the fittest." Defeating your adversary with a sword is one thing, but to vanquish your enemy with a knife and fork is quite another.

YOU CAN'T JUDGE A BOOK…

It is not easy to pick a cannibal from their appearance alone. They won't, as a rule, look any different from your garden-variety omnivore, vegetarian or, for that matter, vegan. They rarely wear shrunken heads around their necks or ladle questionable soups out of blackened cauldrons. Telltale signs are often much more subtle and can be easily missed by the untrained eye. Consider the following:

> Those who denounce cannibalism most vehemently will probably be the first to bring out their knives and forks when the ash hits the fan.

> Watch out for discrete inquiries about your body mass index or surreptitious pinches to your prized meaty bits.

> Be cautious of those who "joke" about being so hungry they could eat a horse and chase the rider. A man-sized appetite may be just that.

> When visiting neighbors, avoid invitations to bathe in any water containing vegetables or smelling, even remotely, of Italian herbs.

If in any doubt, the best course of action is to avoid all dinner invitations as forcefully as possible—preferably with both barrels.

A STITCH IN TIME...

In a time when having a few friends over for dinner may take on a whole new meaning, it is important that we take a few precautions prior to responding to any RSVP.

Always carry an official-looking, forged document, preferably from a doctor or contagious diseases specialist, stating that you have one of any number of extremely nasty ailments. This may be enough to keep you off the evening menu or, at least, give you some time to assess the escape potential from the pit they have thrown you in.

Carry an emergency supply of some tidbit or delicacies that can be scattered as a decoy during a time of crisis. If the treats you've tossed seem more appealing to a cannibal than your left leg, then you may have opened a brief window of opportunity, by way of distraction, for your escape.

Dressing down or not using antiperspirant for six months won't necessarily act as a deterrent to being eaten. Even Cinderella came up a treat with a bit of spit and polish.

If your guest room is a dimly lit dungeon full of foul-smelling amputees, then you can be pretty sure that you are the latest addition to a human feed lot. Make your excuses (preferably accompanied by small arms fire) and get the heck out of there.

Die-hard vegetarians be warned; organically grown, fresh off-the-bone meat will be a highly prized delicacy in the post-apocalyptic world; so ensure that you have a good pair of running shoes and a few extra ammunition clips on hand.

> Remember, when it comes down to it, you don't need to be able to run faster than a cannibal to be off his evening menu, you just need to run faster than the guy next to you.

PANDEMIC

`"I can fix this."`

—ROBERT NEVILLE, *I AM LEGEND*

During the late thirteenth century, Europe was decimated by the outbreak of bubonic plague. The Black Death, as it was known, is estimated to have killed somewhere between 30 and 60 percent of Europe's population.

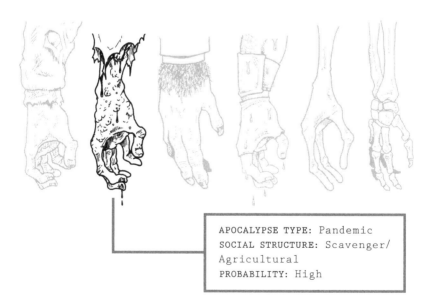

APOCALYPSE TYPE: Pandemic
SOCIAL STRUCTURE: Scavenger/ Agricultural
PROBABILITY: High

These types of pandemics have occurred with frightening regularity throughout history. Smallpox, for example, is estimated to have been responsible for the deaths of between 300 and 500 million people during the twentieth century, while tuberculosis is thought to have killed one-quarter of the adult population of Europe during the nineteenth century. And we won't even mention the millions killed by typhus, cholera, influenza, measles, leprosy and yellow fever, or the recent rise of viral hemorrhagic fevers, SARS, H5N1 (Avian Flu), or the antibiotic resistant "superbugs" that threaten to unleash a second round of some of our historical favorites upon us again. And we will say nothing of the diseases still within animal communities that have yet to make the jump to humans, or those locked up in some frozen lake in the Arctic tundra soon to be melted by global warming. Scientists are even thinking of resurrecting long-dead killer bugs from the grave for research purposes. The Spanish Flu, which killed roughly 40 million people in 1918, is one of the bugs that is on the agenda. And who knows which bugs the military is already working on?

There is no doubt that one of the simplest life-forms on the planet is wholly capable of bringing about the apocalypse. It is not so much a matter of if it will happen, but when.

With that in mind, let us consider lessons from one man who had to face a bit more than a runny nose and a sore throat when the big one came.

Case Study: *I Am Legend* (2007)

This is the third movie adaptation (*The Last Man on Earth* [1964], *The Omega Man* [1971]) of Richard Matheson's 1954 book of the same name. Will Smith plays Robert Neville, a military scientist who is the last human survivor in what is left of New York City after a global pandemic. Three years earlier, scientists had discovered a cure for cancer, but it mutates to form an airborne plague that kills 90 percent of the 6 billion people on Earth. Of the 600 million survivors, only 12 million possess a natural immunity to the disease, while 588 million mutate into vampire-like creatures. These Dark Seekers hunt down and kill the remaining immune population. Outnumbered by these vicious mutants, Robert Neville must use all his wits to survive while trying to find a cure for their disease.

Other Movies to Study: *28 Days Later* (2002), *Children of Men* (2006), *Blindness* (2008), *The Omega Man* (1971), *12 Monkeys* (1995)

RULES OF SURVIVAL: PANDEMIC

Always Follow the Rules

It is a well-established fact that your survival in the post-apocalyptic world will depend on your ability to consistently follow a set of strict, self-imposed rules. These golden rules will not come out of any book or be uttered by some cloaked oracle, but rather, they will be crafted from your personal experiences. Each near miss, wrong turn or close encounter will be a lesson from which you will glean life-saving strategies.

Your rules will be unique to the particular post-apocalyptic situation that you find yourself in. Regardless of whether you face aliens, zombies or cannibals in your post-apocalyptic Valhalla, the same dogmatic adherence to these rules will be absolutely vital to your survival. Rest assured that if you break any of these rules, whether by neglect or misadventure, you are asking just for trouble.

You must, however, be prepared to adapt your rules to changing circumstances. Inflexibility is the first step towards disaster.

Also remember to keep your rules simple. The Lord himself covered all the bases in just Ten Commandments. If you find yourself in a tight situation, the last thing you want to do is try and recall Vol. 2 of the rules, Section 15, Subclause 32.

Watch the Clock

I know, it's easy to lose track of time when you're out shopping for a Picasso at the Metropolitan Museum of Art (remember, everything is free post-Armageddon) or just hanging out with your mannequin

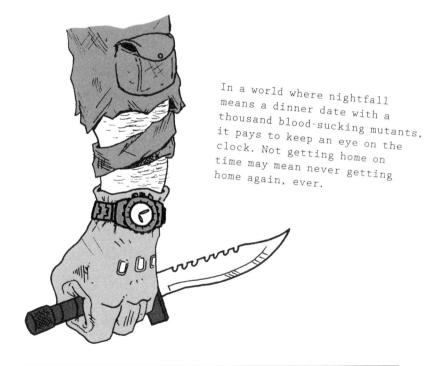

In a world where nightfall means a dinner date with a thousand blood-sucking mutants, it pays to keep an eye on the clock. Not getting home on time may mean never getting home again, ever.

friends. But in a world where nightfall means a dinner date with a thousand blood-sucking mutants, it pays to keep an eye on the clock.

Have a backup watch at the ready in case your primary time-piece malfunctions or is broken or lost, and make sure it has an alarm loud enough to wake the dead; not getting home on time may mean never getting home again, ever.

Avoid the Dark

As obvious as it might seem, it is always surprising how many people ignore this one piece of advice. Bad things happen in the dark. By avoiding the dark, you can effectively cut by half the evils that may befall you outside your secure zone.

Keep Your Almanac Close

If getting home before nightfall is important to you in a world where monsters emerge after dark, then knowing sunset times is of fundamental importance. Ensure that you have an astronomical almanac close at hand, containing year round sunrise and, most importantly, sunset times.

Make sure you give yourself enough time to get from point A to point B and are sufficiently competent to navigate between these two points. Always allow time for unforseen delays and to cover your tracks before retiring for the night.

Be Wary of Mannequins

We all need friends. In a world without people, sometimes you have to settle for whomever you can find. Yet, there are inherent dangers in accepting just anyone into your inner circle. Take mannequins as an example. Although they may seem innocuous enough to the untrained eye, they can be used as a chink in your defensive armor that allows unsavory creatures to take advantage of your social vulnerabilities.

Maybe having one or two as casual acquaintances will not pose too much of a danger. However, it would be wise to avoid establishing a romantic relationship with any mannequin, no matter how attracted you are to them.

If you must have friends, try those of the imaginary variety, or maybe a teddy bear. At least you can keep it with you and make sure that it doesn't get up to any mischief when you're not looking.

If you must have friends, try those of the imaginary variety, or maybe a teddy bear.

... My friends

Keep Your Radio Handy

The radio will remain one of the best ways of advertising your presence in the post-apocalyptic world. It has the potential to extend your search for other survivors over an area of hundreds of square miles rather than just shouting distance. It will also target your search at the right target audience, excluding all those blood-sucking mutants who don't know how to tune a radio dial.

Remember to broadcast on all frequencies and establish a regular meeting point for survivors in an open location.

Avoid Traps

You may not be the only one setting traps in the post-apocalyptic world. Others may be just as interested in catching you as you are in catching them. Booby traps, by their very nature, are often difficult to detect. Always demonstrate caution when traveling through unfamiliar territory or approaching anything that looks remotely suspicious. Don't let your guard down for a moment. Trust your instincts. If a situation looks dangerous, then it probably is. If you sense that something is amiss, carefully retrace your steps and assess the situation. Take an alternate route. You have all the time in the world. There is no point rushing into a situation that could herald your personal end. Never take the direct or easiest approach. Traps are usually set in locations assured of traffic. Take an unconventional route and avoid obvious bottlenecks. Keep an eye out for disturbed soil or vegetation. Enter dwellings via overgrown side doors or windows. If you discover a booby trap, make a hasty retreat. Traps may be under observation by hunters to ensure prey does not escape once ensnared. Remember, being suspended upside-down from your ankle from a classic snare trap as nightfall approaches can end up being significantly more than just an embarrassing inconvenience. It could threaten the future of humanity.

Seal Up Your Home

Your home is your castle. This is never truer than when surrounded by a legion of mutant vampires baying for your blood. If you must stay in an urban area after the holocaust, your primary defense will be in concealing the location of your residence. Once the enemy discovers your home, it is only a matter of time before they get in. Apart from laying a few surprises around the perimeter of your fortress to welcome your uninvited guests (e.g. booby traps, explosives, incendiary devices, etc.), it is vital that you have an escape route planned. Be prepared to abandon your home if necessary. Have a survival kit, weapons and ammo ready to grab on the way out.

Once the enemy discovers your home, it is only a matter of time before they get in.

Set off previously laid booby traps to conceal your escape. Ensure that your exit point is at a suitable distance from your home to avoid detection. Always have alternate accommodation fortified and ready to move into.

PLANET OF THE APES

> "Take your stinking paws off me,
> you damned dirty ape!"
>
> —GEORGE TAYLOR, *PLANET OF THE APES*

Surviving life in the freezer or a cybernetic revolt is one thing. Surviving in a world dominated by our simian ancestors is quite another. Although the chances of the post-apocalyptic dice coming to rest on a world ruled by apes (that is, apart from the human variety) is not high, it always pays to be prepared.

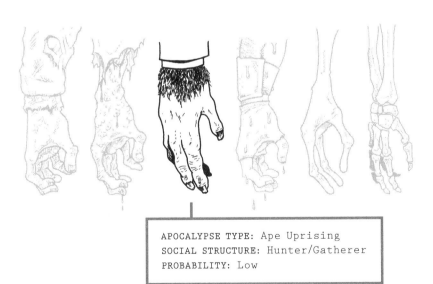

APOCALYPSE TYPE: Ape Uprising
SOCIAL STRUCTURE: Hunter/Gatherer
PROBABILITY: Low

It is the height of human arrogance to assume that we will always be the dominant species on the planet. The vicissitudes of evolution that have seen us ascend to the top of the species pecking order can just as quickly see us kowtowing to "lesser" life forms.

As much as this may offend our delicate sensibilities, it is the harsh law of tooth and nail that determines dominance, not one's high opinions. Our anthropocentric view may have aided our blood-soaked ascendance to global supremacy, but it may also be the chain by which we are dragged screaming into servitude.

Let us hope that our new masters demonstrate more "humanity" to us than we do to the other sentient beings we lord over at present. If our feed-lot concentration camps, conscienceless experimentation and reckless wholesale slaughter of other animals on the planet are anything to go by, then we are in for a very rough time indeed at the hands/claws of another species. As Cornelius, reading from the sacred scrolls, said, "Beware the beast Man, for he is the Devil's pawn. Alone among God's primates, he kills for sport or lust or greed. Yea, he will murder his brother to possess his brother's land. Let him not breed in great numbers, for he will make a desert of his home and yours. Shun him; drive him back into his jungle lair, for he is the harbinger of death." Never a truer word spoken.

Case Study: *Planet of the Apes* (1968)

This film, based on Pierre Boulle's 1963 novel of the same name, follows the story of three astronauts who crash-land on an unknown planet in the distant future. They soon discover that it is ruled by articulate, bipedal apes. Humans are mute, primitive creatures who are enslaved for manual labour and scientific experimentation. One of the astronauts, George Taylor, played by Charlton Heston, escapes from captivity with the assistance of two sympathetic chimpanzees, only to find the half-buried remnants of the Statue of Liberty and other artifacts of a lost civilization. He then realizes that he has not traveled to another star system, as previously thought, but through time to a post-nuclear holocaust Earth.

Other Movies to Study: *Planet of the Apes* (2001)

RULES OF SURVIVAL: APES

Avoid Scarecrows

Scarecrows are scary for a reason; they are designed to keep unwanted visitors away. If, in your exploration of the post-apocalyptic world, you decide to disregard these obvious warnings, then you have no one to blame but yourself if nasty things happen to you.

A general rule of thumb is that the larger the scarecrow, the less enthusiastic are its builders to meet you. Giant effigies made of wood, stone or human body parts should be given a wide berth. If an inspection must be made to satisfy your curiosity, at very least, wait until cover of darkness.

No Skinny-Dipping

When you find yourself in uncharted lands, it is important that you resist the urge to rip off all your clothes at the first given opportunity. Leaving your clothes on the banks of a lake or stream while you frolic nude in the water is just asking for trouble. Not only is there a good chance that they will be stolen by unexpected visitors, but you also face the risk of sustaining an injury while running barefoot trying to recover them. In a world without antibiotics or proper medical attention, even small cuts and abrasions can lead to infections resulting in a slow and painful death.

Also, if the thieves take a liking to you and you find yourself on the run, there is a greater chance of sustaining an injury that will result in your capture.

If you lose your shoes through misadventure, you can fashion primitive footwear from twine and bark stripped from local trees.

Take the Road Less Traveled

If you find yourself in a human stampede being shepherded towards some ugly-looking brutes with fishing nets and truncheons, don't run with the crowd. You have a better chance of avoiding capture if you break free of the mob and make a run for it. Head for cover as quickly as possible. It is always the guy who cowers behind a rock or hides under a log or a steaming pile of corpses that gets away. Leave the battlefield heroics to those who at least have some clothes on.

Feign Stupidity

The last thing you want to do if captured is to stand out from the crowd. Don't do anything that draws attention to yourself. This includes giving your captors any indication that they will need to keep a special eye on you. If they think you are more cunning or intelligent than the rest, they will probably improve security or put you in isolation, making it more difficult for you to escape. You are also more likely to overhear tidbits of information that may aid your escape if they think that you can't understand a word they are saying.

Follow the Dress Code

If on the run, try to blend in as much as possible with the local inhabitants. A skin-tight, silver spandex spacesuit will stand out like a neon beacon, inviting your enemy to single you out for special treatment. Sport the fowl-smelling loincloth, don the

Try to blend in as much as possible with the local inhabitants. A skin-tight, silver spandex spacesuit will stand out like a neon beacon.

macabre leather headdress or rub the odious animal fat over every inch of your body—whatever it takes to make you look like one of the tribe.

Look for Allies

There will inevitably be those in the enemy camp who are sympathetic to your situation. Seek them out, win their trust and provide them with some motivation or benefit for aiding your escape. Watch for telltale signs of kindness, such as providing extra gruel at meal times, ensuring the excrement is regularly cleaned from your cage, or not using a fire hose to separate you from your mating partner.

Cast Your Net

Nets can be hurled by your simian adversary to entangle your limbs while trying to escape or to hold you steady while they bludgeon you with lumps of wood. Apes are much stronger than humans and can throw a net a considerable distance. Avoid passing under low-hanging tree limbs while on the run, and keep an eye on any overhead structures, such as rooftops and bridges. If ensnared, don't panic. Assess the situation and then act. The number of apes surrounding you, your proximity to cover and the nature of any weapons you have at hand will determine what course of action you should take.

Remember, if you choose to acquiesce, any future escape bids will be significantly more challenging.

INTERSPECIES ROMANCE

In the post-apocalyptic world, we are no longer restricted by the social mores and cultural taboos of a civilization that no longer exists. You will define your own moral code and, in so doing, will be free to explore unconventional relationships; if this includes a tryst with an attractive bipedal chimpanzee, then who are we to judge? In a topsy-turvy world where anything goes, a romantic liaison with a primate further down the evolutionary chart than yourself could have many advantages. While an interspecies romance will always raise eyebrows, at very least it may provide you with certain privileges that may enhance your endeavors to escape.

You will define your own moral code and, in so doing, will be free to explore unconventional relationships.

INUNDATION

"Dry land is a myth."

—MARINER, *WATERWORLD*

Mankind is predominantly a terrestrial animal. While half an hour on a rocking boat is enough to get many of us feeling a little green around the edges, imagine a life on the high seas, 24/7. If it can happen to Noah, it can happen to you. Although we may make brief forays into the aquatic environment for work or pleasure, as a species, we are certainly way out of our element. Around 400,000 people drown worldwide every year, with as many as 7,000 drowning in the United States alone (that's about twenty every day). To survive in a solely aquatic environment, it's going to take a little more than just a pair of water wings and some suntan lotion; it's going to take a miracle. All the best miracles are thoroughly prepared in advance.

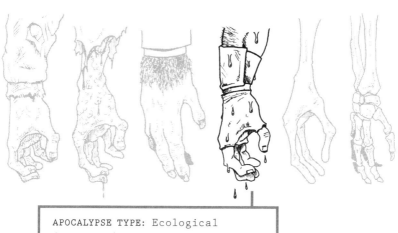

APOCALYPSE TYPE: Ecological
Catastrophe
SOCIAL STRUCTURE: Scavenger/Trader
PROBABILITY: Low

Case Study: *Waterworld* (1995)

In this film, directed by Kevin Reynolds, we find a world engulfed by water after the magnetic poles have reversed and the polar ice caps melted. The remnants of humanity live on floating towns, called "atolls," and survive by scavenging refuse and trading with nomadic seafarers. Kevin Costner stars as the aquatic mutant "Mariner," who battles starvation and outlaws on the high seas after a trading venture turns sour and his genetic heritage is discovered. He flees with the help of a female accomplice and her daughter and eventually finds the last remaining land on Earth.

Other Movies to Study: *2012* (2009), *When Worlds Collide* (1951), *A.I.: Artificial Intelligence* (2001), *The Last Wave* (a.k.a. *Black Rain*) (1977).

RULES OF SURVIVAL: INUNDATION

Prepare to Barter

Post-apocalyptic economies will revert to their most elementary forms. Bartering will rise as the predominant form of trade, where goods and services are directly exchanged for other goods or services without the need of money. Items of most economic value will be those that relate most directly to survival—water, food, ammunition. Those who can secure these prized commodities will attain status and power in any community with which they are associated.

Of course, trade will only take place between people of good will. There will be those only too willing to take what is yours by deception or force. Some brigands may follow the basic principle of bartering by taking your belongings in exchange for your life, but more typically they will just kill you. This solves all the unnecessary worry of you tracking them down for revenge or to reclaim your prized belongings.

Never spend too long at a trading post. The more time you spend around strangers, the greater the opportunity others have of trying to relieve you of your hard-won possessions. Remember, it is your survival that is paramount; the rest can be cut adrift.

Don't Be Choosy

At a time when the basics of life are at a premium, you cannot afford to turn your nose up at the essentials of life, whatever form they may take. Beggars can't be choosers. There will come times when, for the sake of your survival, you will do things that, under normal circumstances, may be distasteful, vulgar or just unappealing in the extreme. Drinking one's own urine, albeit filtered, may be one of them. Sewing an open wound on your leg closed without anaesthetic may be another. The bottom line is, you must do whatever it takes to survive, or you may as well cash in your chips and hope that there's a happy fishing ground in the sky.

Keep a Watchful Eye

Don't expect other survivor communities to welcome you with open arms. They have their own interests to protect, and strangers, like yourself, are always a potential threat to their security. For all they know, you could be a spy reconnoitering their defenses for a surprise attack or there to kidnap their prized female breeding stock. Trust will not be earned quickly.

The more insecure an individual or community is with their personal situation, the greater the degree of xenophobia, or fear of strangers and the unknown. "Stranger danger" is one of the key rules of survival in the post-apocalyptic world.

If your presence is temporarily tolerated for the purposes of trade or information about the outside world, be as cautious of them as they will be of you. Not all danger will be writ large on the fortified walls of their compound. Corpses impaled on spikes like human kebabs will be easy enough to pick, but most signs of danger will be much more subtle.

Listen for expressions like, "The leader says…" or "It is written…" These are usually a sign that the community is living under the tyrannical rule of a deranged megalomaniac or, even worse, fanatical religious zealots who may interpret your arrival as a fulfilment of their prophecy that one day a stranger will arrive who must be sacrificed to appease the wrath of their loathsome god.

Listen for the inadvertent utterances of gormless youngsters, particularly when they are quickly silenced by their elders. A slip of the tongue will more often reveal true intentions than guarded pleasantries. Watch for furtive glances amongst your hosts when you are invited to stay for dinner. They may wish to extend their hospitality in ways that will leave you without the limbs you walked in on.

Keep conversation to a minimum, watch your back, make your excuses and high tail it out of there, if you still can.

Keep Your Cards Close to Your Chest

We all know that people are not always as tolerant and accepting of other's differences as they should be. History is full of conflicts based solely on mere misunderstandings or mindless prejudice in its myriad of forms. In any encounter with survivor communities, it is important to remember that you are at a social and tactical disadvantage. As a stranger, you will not be aware of their protocols or traditions, and it will be easy to transgress unwritten laws or make social faux pas that may offend your hosts. What starts as an innocent inquiry about somebody's mother may quickly escalate into a Mexican standoff, if you are not attuned to the highly strung social dynamics of post-apocalyptic communities.

If you have any distinctive birthmarks, tattoos or mutations, make sure you keep them well hidden. Those of unhinged mind or prone to prejudice may use them as an excuse for relieving you of your possessions or even your life. Wear long hair over those gill

If you have any distinctive birthmarks, tattoos or mutations, make sure you keep them well hidden.

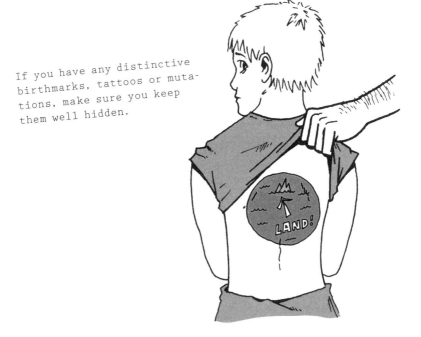

slits behind your ears; a jacket over that map-shaped skin lesion on your back.

Play Your Best Hand

Bluff can go a long way to securing your objective in a tight situation. But if your bluff is called, it is imperative that you can back it up. Hollow words can make your predicament much worse. It is better to act first and talk about it later—that is, if there are any of your enemy still standing.

When in dire circumstances—facing an adversary with tactical superiority in numbers or weaponry, or a hometown advantage—it will take all of your commitment and resolve to survive. No one ever made a splash by testing the water with their big toe; make it a dive-bomb or nothing. Difficult situations call for decisive action. Go in with all guns blazing and damn the consequences. Like the berserkers of ancient Scandinavia, throw caution to the wind and don't hold back. Who dares, wins.

Dress to Kill

It is never more important to dress to impress than in the post-apocalyptic world. Show up in the wrong attire to a post-Armageddon party, and it may be the last one you ever go to. Your appearance must make a statement, and that statement must be that you mean business. Even in the most innocuous of encounters with fellow doomsday survivors, it is important to give the impression that you are not someone to be messed with. Clothing, hairstyle, personal ornaments, piercings/tattoos and demeanor will convey a clear message to those you meet. There will be those just

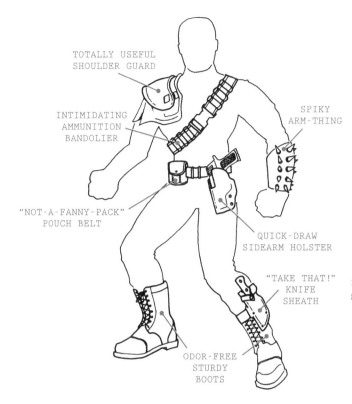

TOTALLY USEFUL
SHOULDER GUARD

INTIMIDATING
AMMUNITION
BANDOLIER

SPIKY
ARM-THING

"NOT-A-FANNY-PACK"
POUCH BELT

QUICK-DRAW
SIDEARM HOLSTER

"TAKE THAT!"
KNIFE
SHEATH

ODOR-FREE
STURDY
BOOTS

It is never more important to dress to impress than in the post-apocalyptic world. Your appearance must make a statement, and that statement must be that you mean business.

waiting to prey on anyone who shows any sign of weakness. Even if you don't have a mean bone in your body, fake it. Bravado can go a long way to acting as a deterrent against aggression. Feigned menace is better than no menace at all.

ALIEN INVASION

"This is not a war any more than there's a war between men and maggots... This is an extermination."

—HARLAN OGILVY, *WAR OF THE WORLDS*

Although aliens may invade our planet via stealth—slowly infiltrating society, one person at a time, with identical pod-people—it is more likely that they will come with heat rays blazing. Such has been the pattern throughout history when superior forces suppress the hapless inhabitants of technologically inferior nations. When heat rays and force fields face projectiles and steel, there is no need for negotiation. Might is right. The glory days of human domination will be over. We have so long subjugated "lesser" species on the planet for our own benefit, that the suffering and torment we cause no longer even crosses our collective minds. When the aliens arrive, we will know what it is like to be on the receiving end of species imperialism. Some might say that it would indeed be poetic justice to see humanity toppled from the summit of the food chain; for so being, we may gain some insight into our own self-centered exploitation of the planet and

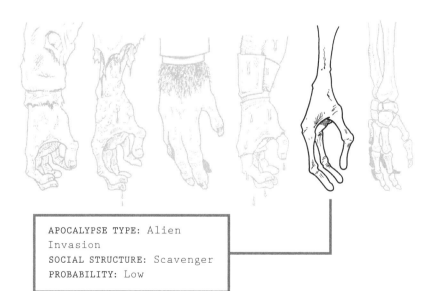

APOCALYPSE TYPE: Alien Invasion
SOCIAL STRUCTURE: Scavenger
PROBABILITY: Low

its myriad creatures. Let's just pray that when E.T. does come, its moral development is at least one rung higher up the evolutionary ladder than our own.

Case Study: *War of the Worlds* (2005)

In this Steven Spielberg-directed adaptation of the classic 1898 novel by H.G. Wells, Tom Cruise plays Ray Ferrier, a New Jersey dock worker who must care for his estranged children while his pregnant ex-wife and her new husband are out of town for the weekend. While struggling with the challenges of parenthood, Ray witnesses the arrival of extraterrestrial beings bent on dominating the earth. Gathering his children, Ray flees the city and heads for Boston, where they can be reunited with their mother. En route, Ray must adopt the uncomfortable role of a father, while playing hide-and-seek with blood-draining aliens and facing an ever-present threat posed by gun-toting refugees.

Other Movies to Study: *Independence Day* (1996), *Invasion of the Body Snatchers* (1978), *The Invasion* (2007), *The Day the Earth Stood Still* (1951, 2008), *Men in Black* (1997), *Mars Attacks!* (1996), *Signs* (2002).

RULES OF SURVIVAL: ALIENS

Watch the Heavens

Unusual atmospheric phenomena may sometimes indicate that aliens are about to attack. If what you're seeing goes against all the physical laws of nature, then you can be pretty sure extraterrestrials are behind it. Strange cloud formations, unusual lightning strikes or even the wind blowing in the wrong direction are all signs to immediately seek shelter.

Listen for any strange or unusual sounds, or a sudden absense of noise altogether, as these may also indicate that an attack is imminent. You don't need to be a rocket scientist to tell that something bad is about to happen. Whirring, thrumming and foghorn blasts from the skies are usually a dead giveaway, but you must also tune your senses to the more subtle signs of danger. Listen for any variation in the sounds coming from alien spacecraft or machinery, including a steady increase in pitch or volume. This usually indicates that they are warming up and could, at any moment, unleash carnage on all around.

Mind the Surge

One of the most serious threats to our ability to fend off an alien invasion comes from the possible use of electromagnetic pulse weaponry against our technological infrastructure. A single high-intensity burst in the upper atmosphere could effectively pull the plug on the United States in an instant, without any direct fatalities. Electromagnetic pulses, or EMPs, create power surges that can fry the electronic systems we are so dependent on in our modern society. Although the military are aware of the hazard and have preparations in place for an EMP attack, civilian targets—including unprotected electrical equipment, communications networks and even entire power grids—are susceptible to widespread failure. Under normal circumstances, repairing the damage could take months or even years. In a post-alien-invasion world, it may never happen. Simply turn the clock back a hundred years to get a picture of what it will be like.

As most vehicles today are highly dependent on electronic circuitry, you cannot assume that you will be able to jump into your SUV to escape the mayhem. You will need to consider other modes of transport. As most city exit roads will be choked by people fleeing the city on foot, try to use alternate routes of escape.

Run Away

Trust your instincts. If something looks dangerous, then it probably is. Millions of years of evolution have provided us with finely tuned hazard receptors. You ignore these at your own peril. Aliens, by their very nature, are out of the ordinary. It is not hard to pick them. They are usually the ones with tentacles, flying around in something that looks like the Guggenheim Museum. Allowing curiosity to override your instinct to "get the heck out of there" is just asking for trouble. Those whose "need to know" outweigh their "need to survive" will inevitably become punctuation marks on the pages of natural selection. If in doubt, look around you. If there are other people running away from something, take it as a sign that you should, too. There is a time and a place for everything. Heroics are best left to those who have nothing to lose. You may come to that point, but make sure it is at a time when your death may actually count for something.

Run like the wind and don't look back.

Stampede

People are fundamentally dangerous. The larger the mass of people in one place, the greater the danger, particularly when they are all heading in the same direction in a confined area. Stampedes are common phenomena amongst large herds of animals, including humans. When spooked, the mass impulse can be to put as much distance between yourself and the perceived danger as quickly as possible. This can often lead to people being trampled to death or asphyxiated. The worst incident of this occurred during a Japanese air raid in Chongqing, China on June 6, 1941. After hearing an "all clear" siren, the citizens of Chongqing left their air raid shelters, but another alarm caused them to turn around and try to get back in again, squashing those still coming out. Approximately four thousand people died as a result.

If caught in a stampede, go with the flow, but try to work your way to one side or the other. Like being stuck in a riptide, it is pointless to try and struggle against the torrent. If worse comes to worst, claw your way to the top of the throng and drag yourself across their heads, like a rock star in a mosh-pit. When on the edge

Masses of people form a focal point for alien attention. Following the crowd makes you an easy target.

of the crowd, take any opportunity to disengage from it and plot a separate course.

Masses of people form a focal point for alien attention. Why pick up individuals with tweezers if you can scoop up handfuls from a crowd? Following the crowd also makes you an easy target for heat rays or being crushed under giant metallic feet.

Run away at 90 degrees to the mob, keep low and head for shelter.

Plan Your Escape

Don't leave it to the last moment to plan your response to an alien invasion. A little bit of preparation now will save a lot of grief in the post-apocalyptic world of red-weed and merciless tripod harvesters. The safest place to be during and after an alien invasion will be

The safest place to be during and after an alien invasion will be away from urban centers.

away from urban centers. Cities will form the focus of the initial alien attack, followed by mop-up operations in smaller towns and rural areas.

Ensuring that you are positioned at a sufficient distance from these harvesting hubs will reduce the risk of detection by both aliens and the refugees who may wish to take advantage of your forethought. Isolated rural or wilderness situations are best. Bear in mind that any above-ground habitation will attract alien eyes.

Remember, during a real alien invasion, the microbe cavalry may not come to our rescue. We may have to fend for ourselves until such time that we can find and exploit chinks in their defenses. So, prepare for the long haul.

Seize the Moment

The adage "he who hesitates is lost" is never truer than when it comes to your interactions with aliens in the post-invasion

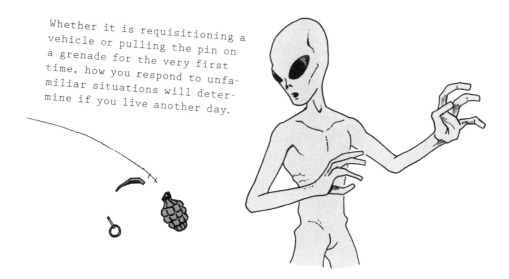

Whether it is requisitioning a vehicle or pulling the pin on a grenade for the very first time, how you respond to unfamiliar situations will determine if you live another day.

world. Sometimes opportunities will only present themselves once, and if you fail to act immediately, both you and your loved ones may perish.

Be prepared to do things that may be outside your comfort zone or field of expertise. Whether it is requisitioning a vehicle or pulling the pin on a grenade for the very first time, how you respond to unfamiliar situations will determine if you live another day. Remember, the meek will not inherit the earth; it will be the one toting the largest laser-blaster.

Create a Circle of Trust

The concept of "stranger danger" is never more an issue than in the post-apocalyptic world. Who you invite into your inner circle may ultimately determine whether you survive or end up skewered on an alien probe, draining you of bodily fluids. Like Doctor Smith in *Lost in Space*, even alleged "friends" can prove to be treacherous.

Before opening the door to any strangers, you must ask yourself what you really know about them. Can what they offer you improve your chances of survival? Are the potential risks greater than the potential benefits? Which of your limited resources are you prepared to share with an outsider? You may be able to look after yourself if things get nasty, but can other members of your group defend themselves?

Remember, guests, like fish, begin to smell after three days. Hospitality can only be extended so far. When their presence becomes more of a threat than an advantage, do not hesitate to do whatever it takes to safeguard your own interests.

Consider very carefully any offers of sanctuary from people wielding guns. Trust your gut instincts; they are usually right.

HOW TO TAKE DOWN AN ALIEN TRIPOD

If Hollywood movies and classic sci-fi literature are anything to go by, then extraterrestrial forces will have the technological advantage when they invade Earth. The tripod-fighting machines first envisaged by H.G. Wells and most recently represented on the silver screen by Steven Spielberg will most probably be protected by some form of force fields. Although, at first glance, this type of defense system may seem impenetrable, a closer inspection will reveal a number of strategic chinks that can be exploited by the prepared backyard guerrilla. If you're not willing to wait and see if terrestrial germs play havoc with the extraterrestrial immune system, here are a few points to consider before launching your attack.

Batter

There is every chance that alien tripods will be protected by an impenetrable energy field. Such fields have long been depicted in science fiction, and if found to be real, could be beyond our technological ability to rupture. If advanced military hardware is incapable of battering its way through, you will have little hope of success using the domestic resources at your disposal. Best to use your brains, not your brawn.

Ensnare

The bigger they come, the harder they fall. If you can find some way of tangling those spindly legs, you may have a chance of bringing one of those big suckers to its knees. This would be no trivial undertaking. The powerful legs of the alien tripods could snap an oil tanker's mooring line like a piece of cotton. Patience, perfect timing and more than a little luck would be required for any chance of success. Don't forget, the Titanic was downed by a lump of ice.

Attack from Below

Attacks from below on a tripod's underbelly may prove more fruitful than direct assaults from outside the tripod's force field. Weapons fired up from between its legs will hit the poorly defended undercarriage of the tripod. Conceal weapons in camouflaged trenches and position bait (one of your disposable comrades) to attract tripods directly over your position. Again, perfect timing will determine the outcome. Make sure your weaponry can be fired remotely.

Infiltrate

If going through it is impossible, then try going around it. If you can bypass the bubble of energy surrounding the tripod, you may have a chance to inflict a mortal wound. Try offering yourself for collection to a food-harvesting tripod. If you are deposited in one of the holding cages along its flanks, you may have a chance to position an explosive or incendiary device into its feeding tube. This will, of course, call for nerves of steel and more than a little luck. If you are successful and survive the fall to the ground without significant injury, head for cover as quickly as possible. Other tripods will be only a foghorn away.

NUCLEAR WAR

"Stay on the path. It's not your concern."
—ELI, *THE BOOK OF ELI*

In a society of such abundance, sometimes it's not possible to appreciate all we have until it is gone. It is easy to lose sight of the fact that what we have can be taken away in an instant, and once

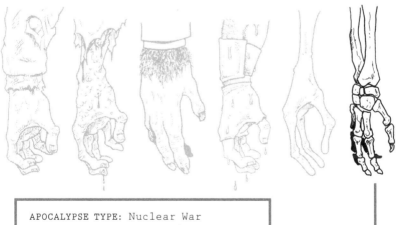

APOCALYPSE TYPE: Nuclear War
SOCIAL STRUCTURE: Hunter/Scavenger
PROBABILITY: High

gone, we may never get it back again. Once the basics of clean water, food and law and order have disappeared, life reverts back to its most basic form: survival of the fittest, or survival of the meanest. While our individual circumstances will go a long way to determining our day-to-day survival in the post-apocalyptic world, our long-term survival will, to a large extent, depend on our will to survive.

For some, survival for the sake of survival may not be enough. There must be a higher purpose, a reason to live. A life without the hope of a brighter future may just not be worth living. From whence may this hope arise? Often from the most unexpected places.

While the bleak, ashen wastelands of *The Road* presented us with one possible outcome of a nuclear war or other such calamity, *The Book of Eli* presents us with a different but equally hellish scenario that must be considered if we are to cover all bases in our preparation for the inevitable.

With the atmosphere stripped bare of its ozone layer and the earth's surface relentlessly fried by UV radiation, survivors must not only face the perils of ruthless highwaymen, but also the challenge of finding a decent pair of sunglasses and moisturizer. For in the land of dry lips, the man with a ChapStick is king.

Case Study: *The Book of Eli* (2010)

Set thirty years after a nuclear war resulted in a "flash" that "ripped a hole in the sky," Eli, played by Denzel Washington, walks west across the barren wasteland that was once America. Holding in his possession a secret book he has guarded for decades, Eli struggles to survive harsh environmental conditions and avoid ruthless brigands who roam the roads in search of hapless travellers.

The only other man who understands the true value of the book is the tyrannical ruler of a small town, who uses everything in his power to take it from Eli. Fundamentally a man of peace, Eli, when challenged, becomes the consummate warrior, fighting to protect the book and ultimately the future hope of humanity.

Other Movies to Study: *Mad Max: Beyond Thunderdome* (1985), *The Day the Earth Caught Fire* (1961)

RULES OF SURVIVAL: NUCLEAR WAR

Where There's Smoke...

Apart from the environmental hazards associated with the end of the world, you will also face competition for limited resources from other survivors. Food, water, fuels, footwear and even ChapStick will all be new commodities of value. Those resources that you do manage to secure for yourself can easily be taken away by those with superior numbers or firepower. Concealing your whereabouts will be the key to avoiding trouble.

Since the very dawn of humanity, fire has been used for cooking, warmth and comfort under the most trying of circumstances. Yet, this one resource, as indispensable as it may be, could be what leads your enemy straight to your door or hole, as the case may be. Smoke can be spotted tens of miles away during the day, and firelight will attract human predators faster than moths to a light bulb at night. Conceal your fire whenever possible.

Smoke can be spotted tens of miles away during the day, and firelight will attract human predators faster than moths to a light bulb at night. Conceal your fire whenever possible.

Keep your fire small and hot. Ensure that your fuel is as dry as possible. Wet wood or leaves create smoke. Try lighting your fire under a bridge or in a cave, a dwelling or a hole in the ground to reduce visibility. Using low-overhead cover, such as a leafy tree, to disperse the smoke will make the plume harder to see from a distance. Ensure your fire is out before moving on.

Avoid Ambushes

It is as easy to be caught in an ambush as it is to set one. Be aware of choke points, such as bridges, tunnels or narrow valleys, both on roads or waterways. Bottlenecks provide your enemy with the opportunity to reduce your chances of escape. Watch for barricades or fallen debris blocking your path and particularly those that fall unexpectedly behind you.

Sometimes an ambusher will endeavor to use bait to lure you into a position that maximizes their advantage. Be cautious if you discover scarce resources, such as food, water or scantily clad women (or men, for that matter) in unexpected places. If you feel uneasy about the path ahead, take an alternate route or find a concealed location to just observe the position for an hour or so. Always err on the side of caution. It is easier to avoid a confrontation than to back out of one once it has begun.

Sometimes an ambusher will endeavor to use bait to lure you into a position that maximizes their advantage. Be cautious if you discover scantily clad women (or men, for that matter) in unexpected places.

Put Your Money Where Your Mouth Is

The post-apocalyptic world will not be for the fainthearted. It will be brutal and unfair. Only those prepared to get their hands dirty will have any chance of survival. This is particularly true when it comes to your interactions with your fellow survivors. There will be times when others will consider their own interests over yours and be only too willing to express their opinions at gunpoint. How you respond to these situations will determine the outcome. If you choose to point out the error of their ways, be prepared for action. It is important that you say what you mean and mean what you say. Either put up, or shut up. You must leave your adversary in no doubt that it was a mistake to cross your path.

But remember to choose your battles wisely. Don't sweat the small stuff. Be prepared to walk away if you can. Every engagement with the enemy exposes you to potential harm. Ask yourself if it is worth it or if there is another way. If so, take it. If not, go in boots and all. Make it swift and merciless. Take no prisoners.

Early to Bed, Early to Rise

Sleeping in could be a thing of the past in the new and exciting post-apocalyptic world. Although sleep constitutes one of the most basic physiological needs, it is also a time in which you are at your most vulnerable. While your sense of hearing stays attuned to a limited degree, there is no guarantee that you will hear your enemy sneaking up on you out of the dark. If you are not alone, take turns keeping watch during the night. When on the move, rise early and be on your way. Cover any traces of your presence as best you can before you leave. Also, resist the temptation to walk on the road. Roads are the focal point for attack by brigands and other unsavory characters.

Be Suspicious

Unsolicited offers of food, water or accommodation should always be viewed with suspicion. Ask yourself what others have to gain by extending hospitality to strangers. Although altruism is not impossible in the post-apocalyptic world, it always pays to be careful. In a world of limited resources, acts of extreme generosity could be motivated by self-interest. Do your hosts look unusually well fed? Is there a backyard full of the graves of other hapless pilgrims? That refreshing drink served in their best china could very well be spiked. To avoid ending up on their evening menu, make your excuses and leave the party early.

Hope Springs Eternal

Where there is no vision, the people perish; this is particularly true in a post-apocalyptic world of anarchy and mayhem. Even in the direst of circumstances, humans have survived unspeakable horrors with just the slightest glimmer of hope. Without the promise of a better tomorrow, there may be little motivation to put in the considerable effort required to survive in a bleak and punishing landscape.

Hope can be derived from a multitude of sources: religious texts, family or the very thought of civilization reborn. Regardless of its origin, humanity's future will be determined by the hopes and dreams that burn within our hearts.

A BRAVE NEW WORLD

Following in the footsteps of our Hollywood legends is but the first step to securing the future of humanity. We have seen how we can gain the edge when it comes to our personal survival by employing the lessons so often taught on the silver screen. Yet our personal survival does not guarantee the continuation of our species. If civilization is to arise from the ashes and once again flourish, we must employ the lessons of history to re-establish a society in which we would want to live. We will be starting at Year Zero, but with discernment, ingenuity and resolve, we can etch our mark on the clean slate of the apocalypse to create a brave new world that surpasses the glories of yesteryear.

SECTION 6

A NEW EARTH

"I know not with what weapons World War III will be fought, but World War IV will be fought with sticks and stones."
—Albert Einstein

Vacations do not always turn out as planned. Sometimes things just don't live up to our expectations. Appalling weather, substandard accommodation, poor service or just plain old bad luck can quickly transform a joyous experience into a holiday from hell. A little more research on your destination prior to departure can often save you a lot of disappointment and discomfort after it. Sometimes simply looking before you leap can save you from hitting rock bottom.

In the same way, the more we envisage the day-to-day practicalities of the new post-apocalyptic world, the better we can prepare ourselves for the unprecedented experiences that await us. As with traveling to a foreign country, the more we learn before we leave, the less our culture shock upon arrival.

To that end, it is important that we now examine some details that will turn what could be just another end of civilization story into a bright new future for humanity. Small things can mean so much when your back is to the wall. A little forethought now will give you the edge when conditions are far from optimal. Your personal survival is practically guaranteed if you put into practice what has been covered so far in this handbook. What follows is for those who wish to do more than just survive; it is for those who want to flourish, for those that see catastrophe as an opportunity, a chance to redress the mistakes of the past and create a new world of your own design.

Doomsday is a time to set your clock back to zero. What has gone before will be no more; what lies ahead is what we make it. But before we remake our world, we must learn the practicalities of living in it.

PERSONAL RELATIONSHIPS

When it comes to relationships and dating in the new world, things start to get a little tricky. While the worst-case scenario may have you hitting on mannequins in your local haberdashery, chances are you'll most likely encounter at least a limited selection of prospective mates from neighboring tribes from time to time. Although the circumstances surrounding these meetings may be far from romantic, it is important that we bear a few important points in mind if we wish to improve not only our dating outcomes but also ensure the survival of our species.

Goodbye Gucci and Armani, hello Mad Max and dumpster diving. Post-apocalypse fashion will be characterized by practicality and procurability, not pretension. In the harsh environment and social conditions of the new world, your primary concern will be extending your tenure on personal existence. To this end, how you look after yourself will ultimately determine your shelf life. If a picture says a thousand words, how you present yourself to other survivors may have a bearing on the outcome of any such encounters.

Go Forth and Multiply

Repopulating the world may seem a little overwhelming to begin with. Don't worry; starting from scratch on any big project can often seem daunting. Just remember, this will be a long-term project and it is not solely your responsibility. You can only do so much to spread your seed across the face of the earth. The rest is up to the fertile soil on which it falls. It's a matter of simple mathematics.

Never Say Never

We all know what happens when we start wading in the shallow end of the genetic pool. We need go no further than some current backwoods communities to find the disturbing effects of inbreeding. Depleted breeding stocks after the apocalypse will make finding a suitable mate more than a little challenging. Although you will need to demonstrate some degree of discernment when choosing mating partners, you cannot afford to be too picky. Forget about compatibility and mutual interests—the ability to handle small arms and to keep up with you when on the run from marauding cannibals will be more important.

Forget about compatibility and mutual interests—the ability to handle small arms and to keep up with you when on the run from marauding cannibals will be more important.

It is important that you never say never. Someone who now has you backpedaling with vigor may in the cold light of a post-apocalyptic dawn seem a little more appealing. Beggars can't be choosers.

Raiding Parties

There is nothing like a good raiding party to instill a bit of genetic diversity into the breeding stock of your community. Although the practice has fallen out of favor in modern society, there may come a time when it—and arranged unions—are deemed a necessity. Whether being raided or doing the raiding, it is important to remember that what at one time may have been socially reprehensible, can soon become the norm when things get tough.

POST-APOCALYPTIC APPAREL

The fashion clock will stop dead on doomsday, at least for a little while. Most of us will stride into the brave new world wearing no more than what we are wearing on doomsday morn. Surviving doomsday and its aftermath will be our priority, and our clothes will attest to that. The focus will be on functionality over fashion. This will include protecting ourselves from environmental extremes and the unwanted attention of other survivors.

As few in our modern society possess the knowledge of how to make fabric, synthetic or otherwise, when our doomsday wardrobe eventually rots from our backs, it will be up to us to use alternative attire. Animal skins will once again come into their own. Leather is hard wearing, versatile and when correctly styled, can provide you with a formidable appearance for your inevitable encounters with other survivors. With field-expedient body armor in place, securely strapped leggings and buckles firmly tightened, you can step out of your bunker and face the perils of the new world with the confidence you're going to need.

However, just because you are on post-apocalyptic skid row doesn't mean that your wardrobe must be devoid of style. Even the most destitute homeless person can exhibit a little flair with a few carefully chosen details. It's the little things that matter. The necklace of human teeth, the folds in your robe that shelter concealed weapons, the spiked shoulder guards—all communicate a clear message to others you meet on the road. (That message is: Don't mess with me.) Going from vagabond into a valiant defender of humanity's future can start with the small vestiges of a hero's attire. Yet, looking like a gladiator won't mean much if you are unable to deliver the goods. But at least it is a start.

Makeup

A few dabs of makeup will go a long way toward hiding the ravages of the harsh post-apocalyptic environment. However, it won't be Revlon or Estée Lauder you'll be reaching for after doomsday. Taking a page from our primitive forebears, we will need to take advantage of whatever we have at hand if we wish to look our best. Start with an animal-fat foundation to keep those pesky mosquitoes and other creepy crawlies at bay. It will also help insulate you from the cold. Using a liberal coating of ash or mud will enhance your natural features. Earthy skin tones will suit all occasions. Remember, makeup can be used to either intimidate your enemies or avoid detection (a person not seen is a person not eaten). Charcoal stripes on your face,

Remember, makeup can be used to either intimidate your enemies or avoid detection (a person not seen is a person not eaten).

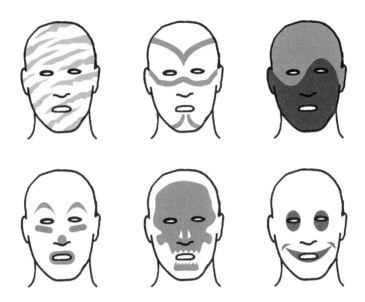

for example, will not only give you that battle-ready marine look, but also make it more difficult for your enemies to spot you as you hide amongst roadside debris. Any tattoos and decorative scarring must be prominently displayed to reveal your tribal allegiances.

Footwear

When your feet are the only thing standing between you and a cannibal's hotpot, it pays to look after them. There is no shame in running away. Most of the great military leaders of history have turned their backs and headed for the hills in what they call a "strategic retreat" at some stage or other. But you won't get far without adequate footwear. Ensure your shoes are sturdy, hardwearing and a good fit. There is nothing worse than getting a blister on your heel while being pursued by a gun-toting pack of mutant hillbillies. Good tread and arch support are essential. Steel caps will give you the edge when sinking the boot into your fallen foe.

As with most things, shoes don't last forever. When shopping for upgrades from the feet of rigor mortis-ized corpses you pass on the road, don't be disappointed if you can't find your exact size. If they don't fit, keep them; you may be able to trade them for some that do.

The stench of death from such acquisitions will also aid you to imitate a corpse as you lie cowering in a ditch when hiding from a torch-bearing mob of rednecks.

Bad Hair Days

With the absence of barbers and hair stylists, life after the apocalypse is guaranteed to be one long succession of bad hair days. Days filled with scavenging for food and avoiding enemies will leave little time for hair care, and with your head kept low, who's going to see it anyway? Matted dreadlocks, mullets and ZZ Top-style beards will be the new standard. Those prepared to undergo the gruelling process of cropping their hair with sharpened rocks will have the advantage when it comes to lice and other vermin.

It must be remembered, however, that if your goal is to restore some semblance of civilization in the new world, no one is going to take you seriously if you have a hairdo like Eraserhead. It must be a standard-issue hero cut, or nothing.

Personal Hygiene

Although you may not have the same social life that you once did, it is important that you do not let yourself go. First impressions

Life after the apocalypse is guaranteed to be one long succession of bad hair days. Matted dreadlocks, mullets and ZZ Top-style beards will be the new standard.

still count, particularly when it comes to meeting potential mating partners. It will not so much be the daily exercise that you will need to worry about or reducing your calorie intake, but the simple personal hygiene issues that make such a difference when getting up close and personal.

For some, the greatest horrors of the post-apocalyptic world will lie with the absence of personal hygiene products. No soap, shampoo, skin care products, toothpaste, medications, ointments, antiperspirant or toilet paper. Toilet paper! Think about it. The post-apocalyptic world will literally stink. The human body, au naturel, is as smelly as any beast of the field. Not only will you have to literally fight for your survival on a daily basis, but you will have to learn to live with your own personal smell-o-rama. What now takes only a few minutes of attention a day and a squirt from an aerosol can or two will, post-apocalypse, consume considerably more time, effort and ingenuity.

Unlike our medieval ancestors, we will not have the luxury of hundreds of years of folk knowledge of herbs and ointments to help us. We will need to reinvent the wheel, or the deodorant, as it were. Those who can mix effective potions with pestle and mortar will be in high demand.

One small advantage of the B.O. apocalypse will be the ability to smell your enemy coming a mile off.

PERSONAL HYGIENE—MEDIEVAL STYLE

Medieval society was no stranger to issues of personal hygiene. A number of health care compendiums written during the Middle Ages recorded home remedies for a variety of garden-variety afflictions, ranging from the perils of halitosis to the social suicide of dandruff. With pharmacies permanently closed for business, you may want to consider some of the alternatives. As it was, so shall it be.

Toilet paper: a cloth or a sponge dipped in water; leaves; or simply the left hand

Toothbrush: a piece of cloth or twig

> **Mouth wash:** a range of herbs including fennel, parsley and mint
>
> **Soap:** boiled down animal fat or olive oil mixed with lye (potassium hydroxide) from wood-fire ash
>
> **Shampoo:** fern-ash, vine-stalks and egg white
>
> **Hair remover:** bean flour, lime, urine and sulphurate of arsenic

COMMUNITY DYNAMICS

There are those who would boldly step into the post-apocalyptic world as lone warriors, independently battling the tide of evil that will encompass the globe. As free agents, accountable to no one, they will have the freedom and flexibility to respond quickly to changing circumstances. Unencumbered by social commitments, they will stand or fall by the might of their own hand, the sharpness of their cunning and the strength of their resolve. For them, the new world will be the edge upon which they test their mettle.

Although wearing the mantle of self-sufficiency may, at times, have its advantages, it is not without its hazards. Humans are communal animals for good reason. Community provides both an emotional and physical support system for the individual. Without it, we are at the mercy of fortune. No man is an island; those who try to be are often submerged beneath the misadventures of life.

The path of the hero may lead in many directions. If yours brings you to community after Armageddon, the following points may help you avoid meeting a dead end.

A Friend in Need…

Those who accompany you on your journey of discovery in the new world will either be a hindrance or an aid to your survival. Apart from family members and friends, you must ask yourself what each individual can contribute toward the betterment of the group. If the answer is nothing, then they should be abandoned. This may not be as easy as it seems. Social convention may lead to some very awkward or tense moments of confrontation. In a lifeboat situation, it is essential that there is some discrimination as to who gets in the boat. If all clamber aboard then all are at risk of going down with the ship. You must be prepared to step on the fingers of those holding onto the side if you are to stay afloat. Hard times call for hard decisions. The post-apocalyptic world is no place for wimps. Remember, your best interests are ultimately the best interests of humanity. So, be strong and put your foot down. Although altruism must always play a part in your decision making, you owe it to humanity's future to ensure, first and foremost, your own survival. There is no better judge than you as to how to achieve that goal.

The Stone Age reality of the new world will present you with untold challenges. Few of us possess the wide range of skills required to meet the diverse situations we will inevitably encounter. Can you set a broken bone, treat an infected wound without antibiotics, pull a tooth without anesthetic, purify water, set a snare trap, grow crops from seed, weave your own clothes or build a fortification that will keep both the chill of a nuclear winter and marauding mutants out? If we are to do more than merely subsist in the new world, we must be prepared to open our arms to those who can contribute to the greater good of our cause.

The knowledge of our forefathers that bestowed them with some degree of self-sufficiency has now largely been lost. One hundred years ago, things were significantly different. People had to look after themselves. As part of a consumer society, we now rely almost wholly on mass-produced manufactured goods designed for our convenience, not our independence. Multinational corporations and governments pull the strings that determine the course of our lives. We are spoon fed and tethered to technologies that bind us to an economic system that now, even before the apocalypse, teeters on the brink of collapse. When our life support system is cut off, those with traditional knowledge and skills will be highly valued. Just like now, your success in the post-apocalyptic world may to a large extent rely on who you know. Invite your dentist and local co-op farmer over for a barbeque this weekend.

HAVE GUN, WILL TRAVEL

The importance of weapons in the post-apocalyptic world cannot be overemphasized. Without the protection of a civil security forces to police law and order, it will be every person for himself. Imagine the Wild West without the sheriff to come to your rescue, and you have some idea of what it will be like. We need go no further than recent natural disasters to see what happens when people are not restrained by the rule of law. Countries already awash with firearms, such as the United States, will have the most to worry about when 911 is no longer an option. A lock-and-load culture will see those unprepared to reinforce their opinions with the barrel of a gun at the mercy of those that are.

Conflict Resolution

Conflict is inevitable. Limited resources have a way of bringing out what lies at the very heart of humanity: self-preservation. This is a genetic imperative that has seen the fittest survive the most miserable of circumstances since the very dawn of time. When bad goes to worse, how you respond to conflict will determine whether you survive to scavenge another day. Conflict resolution will consist of an open and frank exchange of gunfire. Those who can express themselves most articulately with lead will have the upper hand.

The Meek Will Not Inherit the Earth

At first you will probably be reluctant to take human life. This is an understandable. Most of us are conditioned since birth to respect the personal existence of others. We tend to frown on those cultures that do not hold our own opinions on the sanctity of life. Yet, we do not hold all life in the same high regard. It is easy to forget that unless you are a vegetarian, you are already part of an institutionalized killing machine. Do you give a moment's thought to the concentration camp living conditions and terror-stricken deaths of the animals you eat? No. Do you bat and eyelid when you consider the countless animals that have laid down their lives so you can thoughtlessly enjoy your burger or kebab? Not at all. Your heart is already hardened and you don't even realize it. All you need to do is transfer the deep lack of empathy that you already have to your own species and you'll have what it takes. Once the intellectual hurdle of taking human life is overcome, your chances of survival rise exponentially.

The Quick and the Dead

Shoot first; ask questions later. Those who cannot live by this adage may find they have a very short shelf life in the fast and furious post-apocalyptic world. He who hesitates in a critical situation could very well find himself served with gravy at his adversary's evening meal. Your survival will depend on your ability to quickly read a situation and respond with appropriate and forceful action. Learn to trust your gut instincts; if a situation seems bad, it's probably a lot worse. The speed of your reflexes will either make your day or someone else's.

Have a Plan B

Always carry one or more backup weapons. Loss of your firearm, mechanical malfunctions or lack of ammunition could find you in more than just an embarrassing situation. Never underestimate the potential of field-expedient weapons; in

Your survival will depend on your ability to quickly read a situation and respond with appropriate and forceful action.

the right hands, a sharpened pencil or coffee machine can kill someone just as effectively as 9 mm Beretta. Retain the element of surprise by cunningly concealing a number of different weapons about your person.

Location, Location, Location

Initially, isolation from other survivors of the apocalypse will be the key to your community's survival. The period immediately after doomsday will be most dangerous. As civilization disintegrates, society will degenerate to its most primitive form. Driven by hunger, the multitudes will sweep across the land like a plague of locusts devouring the last remaining food stocks. Those who stand in their way will be cut down with no more consideration than hyenas feeding on the still-writhing body of an antelope. Desperation will drive normal people to do things that would be unthinkable under ordinary circumstances. The most prudent strategy is to be as far away as possible from the madding crowd. Fortifications and arms will only go so far toward protecting your hard-gained resources. A committed raiding party is not easily stopped, particularly if well armed and with superior numbers. Not being found will be first defense for your community. But it will also present you with considerable challenges.

Ideally, you should locate your community in an isolated rural or wilderness location. A site with access to clean water, arable land and grazing area for livestock will be preferable. Sites close to waterways have many advantages. Apart from a ready access to fisheries and sea food (in the case of the ocean), they conceal access to your community. Roads and trails always lead somewhere. If your community can be accessed by either, then it will only be a matter of time before bloodthirsty desperados find you. Competent, highly motivated trackers will easily detect attempts to conceal or camouflage roads or paths leading to your community. Waterways leave no trace of your coming and going. Ensure landing areas are adequately concealed and your habitations are a sufficient distance away from the shore to avoid detection. If surrounding terrain or vegetation is unconducive to overland approaches, waterways may be the only practical approach. Establish observation posts with rostered sentries to keep a look out for trouble.

How to Find a Stash

Fuel, ammunition, food and other scarce resources will be in high demand after the apocalypse. After shops and warehouses have been looted and private residences ransacked, you are going to have to employ some lateral thinking to find what others have squirreled away. Caches will not be easy to find. However, your very survival may, on occasion, depend on you doing so. You must expect that others are going to be as creative and cunning at concealing their personal stashes as you are. Your chances of winning the game of hide and seek will increase if you bear the following in mind:

Ask yourself, "Where would I hide it?" If they are as smart as you, there's a good chance of it being there.

Avoid an unnecessary waste of time by examining "the last place you'd look" first.

Look carefully for any signs of disturbance. Broken vegetation, loose floorboards, drag marks or freshly dug earth may all indicate recent activity. Few people are skilled enough to conceal all telltale signs.

Listen for hollow sounds beneath your feet; there could be an underground bunker or storehouse full of supplies just inches below your steel-capped boots, waiting to be discovered.

Beware of booby traps. Hoarders are probably just as keen to keep their stash out of your hands as you are to get them on it.

Target locations more likely to have hidden stockpiles, such as the backwoods cabins of survivalists or members of The Church of Jesus Christ of Latter-day Saints (members are encouraged to stockpile at least six-months supply of food and other consumables for times of trouble). Ensure premises are unoccupied prior to entering.

Hiding Your Stash

There are few things more annoying than going to all that trouble of putting together a decent cache of food and essential supplies only to have them stolen by someone who believes that their own survival is more important than yours. A little bit of forethought can go a long way towards protecting your interests from prying eyes and shovels.

Aim to make finding your stash as difficult as a needle in a hay stack. Try burying your cache in out-of-the-way places, such as a forest or in the mountains. If in the open, place sufficient dirt over the hole to avoid that hollow sound when stepped on. Preferably dig a hole in a concealed location where access is difficult, such as in thick scrub or under a pile of debris. Caches are like car keys: It's important to remember where you put them. Memorize local landmarks; count the number of steps from nearby geographical features; draw a map. If an X marking the spot worked for pirates, it will work for you.

Closer to home, if you really want to put them off, conceal your stash under a pile of contaminated bodies or in a sewage system. Make sure you use a suitably sealed container to store your gear, and wear protective gloves and clothing when accessing it; in a world without antibiotics, you can't risk getting an infection in that small cut on your left pinky.

Remember, the last place they would look should be the first place you hide it.

LOOTING FOR DUMMIES

Sacking, plundering, pillaging, looting. Call it what you will, but theft will be widespread after doomsday. The period immediately after D-Day will be characterized by panic and desperate efforts by the ill-prepared to secure provisions. Of course, at this time, you should already be ensconced in your well-stocked wilderness retreat, but if circumstances find you in a less than ideal situation, you may need to consider the merits of taking that which does not belong to you.

While the gormless majority will initially target electronic goods, home furnishings and other such obsolete consumer items, those with a little more discernment will head for food and fuel. More astute looters will focus their attentions on items of long-term value, such as nonperishable foods, arms and ammunition, alternative power equipment, medicines, horticultural provisions and items relating to a self-sufficient, sustainable lifestyle.

Expect a high level of competition for valuable items. Avoid locations that are being looted by others. Demonstrate extreme caution looting private premises; even dwellings that seem abandoned may be concealing a lot more than a few previously overlooked items in the pantry. Others will probably go to the same extent as you to protect their assets.

If you must go in, ensure that you have observed the premises for an extended period and reconnoitered the surrounding area for signs of habitation. Watch out for booby traps.

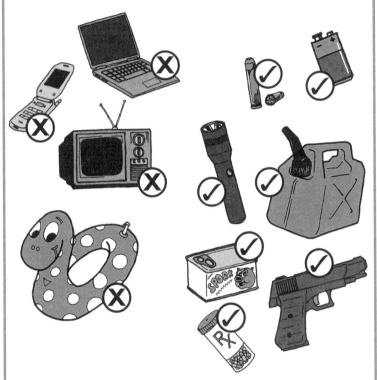

More astute looters will focus their attentions on items of long-term value, such as nonperishable foods, arms and ammunition, alternative power equipment, medicines, horticultural provisions and items relating to a self-sufficient, sustainable lifestyle.

A Kingdom of Your Own

No kingdom is complete without a king. As the Bard said, "Some are born great, some achieve greatness and some have greatness thrust upon them." If the burden of responsibility falls upon your broad shoulders, you owe it to what is left of humanity to get it right. The form of governance you adopt in your community may determine its long-term viability. It's all very well to espouse the virtues of the democratic process within the controlled environment of a parliament or congress, but when the rubber hits the road, a more decisive form of government may be called for. All that tedious messing around with ballots and review committees may just get in the way when gun-toting brigands have breached your perimeter defenses. Modern history has demonstrated that not all societies are at a stage where democratic processes best suit their needs. In the absence of a civil society, sometimes it is necessary for a more stringent approach to ensure the wheels stay on the wagon. Times of crisis call for action, and action requires someone who can get the job done without the interference of those who can't. If that person is you, then you owe it to yourself and the future of humanity to step up to the plate.

We have many models of government from which we can choose that will help keep you at the top of the chain of command. From tribal chieftainships to hereditary monarchies, authoritarian to totalitarian dictatorships, the world is your oyster in terms of lording it over your minions. This is your chance to show them how it should be done. It's easy enough to say "If I were in charge, this is how I'd do it," but actually doing it can be more than a little difficult. Leadership, particularly in a time of crisis, is fraught with many challenges. If you want to stay ahead of the game, be prepared to lead by example and learn quickly from your mistakes.

WHAT'S THE BIG IDEA?

Where there is no vision, the people perish. As a newly established leader, it is important that you provide a reason for being, besides mere survival. Although hardwired into the genetic code of all living creatures, survival for survival's sake may not be enough incentive to endure the trials of the post-apocalyptic world. People are united by a common cause and are more willing to brave hardship if they think there is some purpose for doing so. As possibly the last bastion of civilization in a decimated world, your community must have a collective dream to sustain it through the inevitable post-apocalyptic tribulations.

Your community must have a collective dream to sustain it through the inevitable post-apocalyptic tribulations.

WHAT'S IN A NAME?

The post-apocalyptic world is the perfect environment in which to reinvent yourself. You can become anyone you want to be, within limits. (Exclude day-trader, insurance salesperson, etc. Well, when you come to think of it, most jobs actually). The slate is wiped clean. There is no need to restrict yourself to the mundane name with which you were born. Like leaders from the past, you can assume a title that is more befitting your newfound position of authority. Who was Ivan Vasiljevich before adding "the terrible" to his name, or young Vlad Dracula before becoming Vlad the Impaler? It can be as simple as adding "the Great" to your Christian name; just look at where it got Alexander, to name but one.

Alternatively, you can adopt a more minimalist approach like Hitler, Stalin or Oprah (now there's a trio you don't see very often) and abbreviate your name to its shortest form. Bear in mind that your name should encapsulate the image you wish to convey to

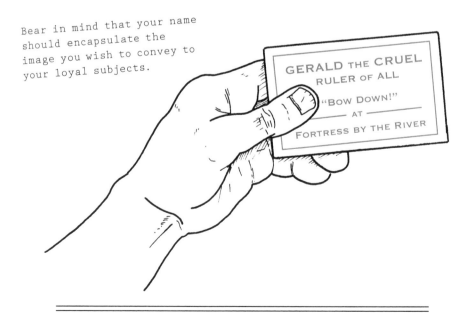

Bear in mind that your name should encapsulate the image you wish to convey to your loyal subjects.

GERALD THE CRUEL
RULER OF ALL

"BOW DOWN!"

— AT —

FORTRESS BY THE RIVER

your loyal subjects. Be creative. If all goes well, your name will last a lot longer than you do and oft fall with hallowed reverence from the lips of your devoted followers.

The power to allocate names does not stop at your own. Just as Adam named the beasts of the field, you too can rename all that lies within your domain. This is your chance to right the many absurdities of the English language and create a language that befits the parameters of the new world in which you find yourself. Start with your immediate vicinity. Following in the footsteps of previous leaders, you can name your village/hamlet/bunker after yourself by simply adding a suffix such as -town, -ton, -ville or, if you're feeling particularly adventurous, -grad or -berg, for that old-world feeling of indomitability. Heck, you may as well rename the whole country. It's as easy as adding -ia to the end of your name. Try "Latinizing" it for added solemnity.

CHAIN OF COMMAND

Henry Longfellow once said that, in this world, a man must either be an anvil or a hammer. If it has fallen upon you to be a hammer, you should grasp the handle with both hands and swing away. A time of crisis calls for decisive leadership. The future of your community will depend on your ability to make executive decisions at a moment's notice. As the commander in chief of your new empire, the buck stops with you. This is your time to shine. Yet no general fights his battles alone. Success or failure depends as much on selecting the right people for the jobs under you as it does upon the decisions you make. General Douglas MacArthur said that "a general is just as good or just as bad as the troops under his command make him." It is imperative that you choose carefully those who would assist you to guide your community through the troublesome times that will lie ahead of you.

WATCH YOUR BACK

Establishing your empire may be the easy part; keeping it intact may prove more challenging. All leaders invariably have seditious blaggards lurking in the shadows, just waiting for an opportunity to pounce and seize power for themselves. Treachery goes with the territory; for every Caesar there is a Brutus. Often the greatest threat comes from those you know best and suspect least. If you want to avoid having others rain on your parade, you will need to keep a close watch on those around you. A little paranoia goes a long way toward nipping insurrection in the bud. Pre-emptive strikes are a sign of a leader at the top of his game. Don't let relationships cloud your judgement. Some members of your community may have to be banished (or worse) to protect the integrity of your position. As the British Liberal Party leader Jeremy Thorpe, once declared, "Greater love hath no man than this, to lay down his friends for his life."

DON'T BITE OFF MORE THAN YOU CAN CHEW

It's one thing to be head honcho of your own community, it is quite another to rule over an empire that stretches beyond the field of your vision. You'll have quite enough to worry about initially without spreading your resources too thinly. Remember, some of the greatest empires the world has ever known have collapsed because they extended their reach beyond what they could manage. Although there will be no better time for a land grab than in the aftermath of the apocalypse, you should resist the temptation to acquire too much real estate. Concentrate on your immediate vicinity. There will be plenty of time for empire building later.

CREATING RELIGION

Having eluded marauding cannibals/zombies/robots and endured untold hardships to forge a small bastion of civilization in the bleak wastelands of a decimated world, the last thing you want is to have it wrested from your hands by some act of treachery by your minions. Without your sure hand at the helm, not only is the future of your community imperilled, but the entire future of humanity.

If history has taught us anything, it is that those who wish to secure their position at the top of the decision-making hierarchy can best do so by securing the hearts and minds of the people. To this end, the judicious use of religion has proved unparalleled as a tool of control. Few civilizations have been built without the guiding hand (or fist) of those with a direct line to the gods.

And what better way to begin the new age than by starting your own religion? If it worked for L. Ron Hubbard, it can work for you. With a little imagination and planning, you can create a spiritual empire to match those of the Aztecs or Ancient Egyptians.

Flights of Fancy

Drawing up the blueprints for your new religion will be a time to unleash your creativity and let your imagination go wild. There is nothing you could dream up that is so ridiculous that your followers will not be prepared to believe. Just look at the world's great religions. In fact, the more absurd or unbelievable your mythology, the more your followers will devote themselves to it. You need not even start from scratch; most religions are founded on those that precede them. Feel free to appropriate ideas from other sources: movies, literature, the instructions on the side of a packet of instant pudding. Don't forget, all copyrights expired on doomsday. Don't worry if there are major inconsistencies, contradictions or downright falsehoods; they are there to test the believer's faith. Religion is about the big picture, not the details. It is about soothing reassurances in the face of the horrors of existence, not the facts.

The Good Book

All good religions require a sacred text. Your community must believe that your book is supernatural in origin. It may either be transcribed from a personal vision or penned directly by a deity of your choice or creation. This holy book will form the basis of your religion, being an inerrant source of information, moral instruction and guidance for the faithful. Most importantly, it will establish your authority to rule. There can be no argument against the edict, "It is written."

Sacred Objects

Holy relics need not be elaborate. They can be as simple as the holy flip-flops you wore while standing before your fictional god to receive the holy text, or the piece of charcoal with which you wrote it. They must, however, be deeply woven into the fabric of your mythology. They must be capable of standing alone as icons of your religion, as they may eventually be worshiped in their own right by the faithful.

Holy relics need not be elaborate. They can be as simple as the holy flip-flops you wore while standing before your fictional god to receive the holy text.

Hallowed Ground

All religions have their sacred places. The Jews have the Temple Mount, the Muslims have Mecca and the Sikhs have the Golden Temple in Amritsar. It should be a place where a significant event occurred in your mythology, or a place that is foretold to be the location of a significant event in the future. Your most sacred places should be inaccessible to all but the very elect. Great solemnity and reverence should accompany any visitations.

Branding

All organizations need a symbol or logo which is instantly recognizable. Think Christianity, think the cross. Think McDonald's, think the golden arches. The image will be drawn from your mythology and should convey some sense of menace. Keep it simple and easily

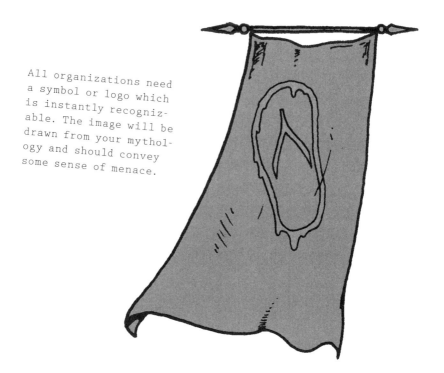

All organizations need a symbol or logo which is instantly recognizable. The image will be drawn from your mythology and should convey some sense of menace.

replicated; it will oft be scrawled in blood to mark the boundaries of exclusion zones (e.g. the entrance to the cave where you hide your secret personal stash) or carved from wood or stone to act as a focal point for worship in the home.

Rituals

Apart from creating a sense of group identity, regular symbolic acts serve to create social bonds that will strengthen your hold on power. A community that prays together stays together. Social cohesion will also unite your community against infiltration or attack by outsiders (a.k.a. unbelievers).

Never underestimate the power of theatrics in rituals and ceremonies. Costumes, music and the use of sacred items go a long way toward creating a sense of occasion in the mundane. Develop "secret ceremonies" for your most trusted members to provide them with a sense of privilege.

Us and Them

It is important to establish a clear distinction between your community and those other survivors that are not of your community. The "us and them" principle has served other religions admirably since the very dawn of the human imagination. Your community must come to view itself as an exclusive group, handpicked by the gods to fulfill a sacred purpose. They are the remnant who have survived the apocalypse by divine protection. Their destiny to inherit the new Earth is now fulfilled, and from them a new and glorious civilization will spring forth. All others are cursed of god. The xenophobia this dogma produces will not only cement the bonds within your community but also help to consolidate your hold on power.

Commandments

Originating from a supernatural source and recorded in your sacred text, the law will provide your community with the definitive guide to correct living within the community. Prescribed conduct and punishments will be outlined in a succinct, authoritative form. Of course, as interpretation of the sacred text ultimately lies with you alone, there is flexibility to accommodate any unforeseen events or, alternatively, to receive further light on the issue from a higher source. Transgression of the law must be met with swift and public punishment. But remember, as Sophocles said, what you cannot enforce, do not command.

Unbelief

Both unbelief and dissension must be met with suitable force. Expel the unbeliever. Banish those who dare to question your authority; cast them into outer darkness, where yea verily they will walk the gray wastelands of the earth forever, amen.

Miracles

The further removed we are from the age of technology, the easier it will be to astound your followers with miracles. Eventually, like time travelers hoodwinking cave-dwellers, the miracle of fire may

Banish those who dare to question your authority; cast them into outer darkness, where yea verily they will walk the gray wastelands of the earth forever, amen.

suffice, even if it is only from small, red-capped pieces of wood. But until then, point out more subtle miracles, such as their survival of the apocalypse and how your guidance is their ultimate gift from the gods.

Prophecy

Prophecy is always best written in retrospect; specific details can then be given. Believers can be told it was written prior to the prophesied events. If future events must be foretold, keep details to a minimum. Write in such a way that there can be multiple interpretations of the text. If a specific prophesied event fails to take place, tell your believers that the gods have smiled upon them and it has been postponed. Their faith and fervent prayers have delivered them. Either way, you win.

Just Desserts

A little motivation goes a long way. Tell your followers of the many advantages that unending devotion will bring during the trials of their daily lives. These daily benefits will pale into insignificance compared to the rewards that await them in the afterlife. No one can definitely disprove that which cannot be seen. Even those who doubt are more likely to cover their bases and play along. Every apocalypse has a silver lining.

Surely Thou Art a God

Why be content with being God's representative on Earth when you can become a god? There is little point sharing the glory with some celestial big brother when you know that it rightfully belongs to you. Self-deification is not as hard as it may first seem. Religion has always been about marketing. Becoming a god in the eyes of men is really no more difficult than getting them to believe in invisible gods that live in the sky. It's all just smoke and mirrors. If it worked for Caligula, it can work for you.

THE END. NO, REALLY.

Things may not always be as bad as they seem; sometimes they can be a lot worse. If the fate of humanity has been predestined and the end envisaged by the Maya is delivered on December 21, 2012, then there is not much we can do about it. Yet we need not despair. Humanity has always been defined not so much by the challenges it encounters, but by the way it responds to those challenges. If it has survived to this point, then there is more than a good chance that it will survive the "end of the world" in some form or other. Whether you personally will be a part of the post-apocalyptic experience will depend on many factors. Whether you would want to survive is another thing. The post-apocalyptic world will not be for everyone. Whether you decide to walk the ashen remains of Earth as a lone Clint Eastwood hero archetype or hunker down and establish a community from which civilization may be reborn, it is up to you. Like no other time will you hold the course of your own destiny in your hands. Timing in life is everything. The post-apocalyptic world will either be your time to shine or for your sun-bleached bones to be scattered amongst the tangled mass of the billions who either didn't make it or decided to just give up. Those who endure will not let a little thing like the End of All Things get in their way.

It will be just a minor setback. Many opportunities are born out of adversity. Those who have the vision to see those opportunities are usually the ones who can see them to fruition.

If nothing happens on December 21, 2012, it does not mean that it never will. It has simply been postponed. Our universe is governed by the laws of entropy. All good things eventually come to an end. Whether we perish vaporized during an asteroid impact or in an accident driving home after doing the shopping, the end eventually comes to us all.

If the clock strikes midnight, December 22, and we are all still here, we can give a collective sigh of relief and continue with our little lives. At least through contemplation of the world's end, we will have been given the opportunity to reassess the things that are most important in life.

If the Maya were correct and the fuse is fizzling its way towards our oblivion, then we have, within the pages of this book, the collected wisdom of the ages that will help make the End of Days not only bearable, but the first chapter of glorious new but different future for humanity. In the end, whether the apocalypse happens or not on December 21, 2012 is not the important thing; it's being ready for it that counts.

APPENDIX

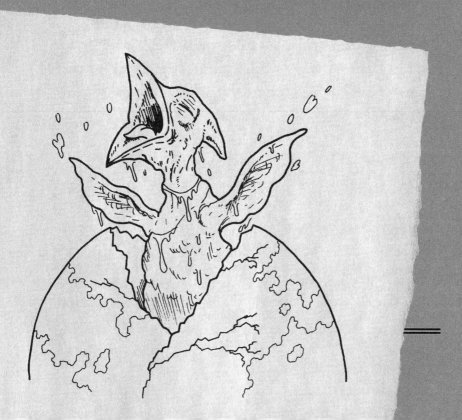

COUNTDOWN
TO OBLIVION

Can you remember a time when as a child, or maybe even as recently as last year, you would count down the days to Christmas or your birthday? Your excitement would build exponentially as the highlight of the yearly calendar slowly approached, until finally the big day arrived and you leapt out of bed at the crack of dawn to open your presents.

With the End of All Things at hand, how much more important is it to keep tabs on how many more sleeps there are to the apocalypse? Nobody wants the embarrassment of being caught with radioactive ash on their face and their metaphorical pants down when they stumble out of bed unprepared on doomsday. Your survival may very well depend on the action plan that you initiate today. Use this Doomsday Planner as a guide to prepare yourself for the inevitable collapse of civilization.

My Survival Equipment Checklist:

_____

_____

_____

_____

_____

_____

Post-Apocalyptic Creature Comforts That I Just Couldn't Live Without:

_____

_____

_____

_____

_____

Possible Underground Bunker or Back-Country Cabin Locations:

_____

_____

_____

_____

_____

Friends, Family Members and Skilled Professionals Acquaintances With Whom I Would Like to Share my Fortified Compound:

_____

_____

_____

_____

_____

Things to Do to Prepare for the Apocalypse Now:

_____

_____

_____

_____

_____

_____

Things to Do One Week Before Doomsday:

_____

_____

_____

_____

_____

_____

_____

_____

Things to Do on Doomsday:

_____

_____

_____

_____

_____

_____

_____

_____

My Short but Heartfelt Speech to Inspire Fellow Survivors as We Prepare to Face the Perils of the Post-Apocalyptic World:

_____

_____

_____

_____

_____

_____

_____

POST-APOCALYPTIC JOURNAL

When written communication goes from Facebook and Twitter to campside oration and petroglyphs in one afternoon, the only records of human experience during this trying period may come from just a handful of scribes. Most survivors will be too occupied with continuing their day-to-day existence to even contemplate jotting down their thoughts for prosperity. Like Samuel Pepys's diary in the 1660s, your journal may become an important primary source for future historians. It could also, depending on the spin woven around your post-apocalyptic experiences, form the basis of a sacred text for future generations. Use this journal space to start your entries.

Day 1, Year 1

_____

_____

_____

_____

Day 2, Year 1

_____

_____

_____

_____

Day 3, Year 1

_____

_____

_____

_____

Day 4, Year 1

_____

_____

_____

_____

Day 5, Year 1

_____

_____

_____

_____

Day 6, Year 1

_____

_____

_____

_____

Day 7, Year 1

_____

_____

_____

_____

INDEX

Also by W.H. Mumfrey...

The Alien Invasion Survival Handbook

Aliens are among us. While the true intentions of these mysterious intruders from outer space are unknown, there's no doubt that their actions are nefarious. Isn't it time you learn how use your MP3 player to defend yourself from their paralyzing powers? Shouldn't you know how to evade the pursuit of a flying saucer? Wouldn't you sleep better at night knowing some proven hand-to-hand combat techniques guaranteed to stop your extraterrestrial foe in its tracks? Make no mistake—our world is under attack and this handbook may be the only thing standing between the human race and total annihilation.

#Z2511, 224 pages, paperback, ISBN: 978-1-60061-162-9

Find this book and many others at MyDesignShop.com or your local bookstore.